ADVICE TO A YOUNG CHRISTIAN

ADVICE

TO

A YOUNG CHRISTIAN

ON
THE IMPORTANCE OF AIMING
AT
AN ELEVATED STANDARD OF PIETY

JARED B. WATERBURY

WITH
AN INTRODUCTORY ESSAY
BY
ARCHIBALD ALEXANDER

SOLID GROUND CHRISTIAN BOOKS
BIRMINGHAM, ALABAMA USA

Solid Ground Christian Books
715 Oak Grove Road
Birmingham, AL 35209
205-443-0311
sgcb@charter.net
http://solid-ground-books.com

ADVICE TO A YOUNG CHRISTIAN
*On the Importance of Aiming
At an Elevated Standard of Piety*

Jared Bell Waterbury (1799-1876)

Solid Ground Classic Reprints

First printing of new edition June 2006

Taken from the 1843 edition by The American Tract Society, NY

Cover work by Borgo Design, Tuscaloosa, AL
Contact them at nelbrown@comcast.net

*Special thanks to Ric Ergenbright for permission to use
the image on the cover. Visit him at ricergenbright.org*

ISBN: 1-59925-076-4

CONTENTS.

	PAGE.
Preface,	5
Introductory Essay, by Rev. Dr. A. Alexander,	7

LETTER I.
Forming an elevated Christian character, . . . 27

LETTER II.
Temptations peculiar to the young Christian, . 33

LETTER III.
Danger of backsliding, ... 38

LETTER IV.
On prayer, ... 43

LETTER V.
On prayer—continued, ... 48

LETTER VI.
Sincerity in prayer, ... 53

LETTER VII.
Faith essential to prayer, ... 58

LETTER VIII.
For what should we pray? 63

LETTER IX.
When should we pray? 68

LETTER X.
The subject of prayer concluded, ... 73

LETTER XI.
On self-examination, ... 78

LETTER XII.
Self-examination, stated and occasional, . . . 83

LETTER XIII.
Superficial self-examination, ... 88

CONTENTS.

LETTER XIV.
The same subject continued, ... 93

LETTER XV.
Danger of deceiving ourselves, ... 97

LETTER XVI
Relying on past experiences, ... 102

LETTER XVII.
Self-examination—continued, ... 107

LETTER XVIII.
Self-examination respects feeling and conduct, . . 112

LETTER XIX.
Frequent and close self-examination, ... 116

LETTER XX.
Stated times of self-examination, ... 120

LETTER XXI.
Preparation for the Lord's supper, ... 124

LETTER XXII.
The perusal of the Scriptures, ... 128

LETTER XXIII.
Religious literature, ... 133

LETTER XXIV.
A systematic perusal of the Scriptures, . . . 137

LETTER XXV.
A careless perusal of the Scriptures, ... 142

LETTER XXVI.
The historical and doctrinal parts of Scripture, . . 147

LETTER XXVII.
The Bible not to be studied for criticism, . . . 151

LETTER XXVIII.
Religion the business of life, ... 155

LETTER XXIX.
Influence of religion on the social relations, . . . 160

Conclusion, ... 16

PREFACE

To the lambs of Christ's flock, whom Peter was enjoined by the Good Shepherd to feed, I dedicate this little book. The letters which compose it were written to instruct one of their number, the daughter of a highly valued friend. Since they are now made public, it is the ardent prayer of the author, that they may comfort and edify many more.

As revivals of religion have become so frequent, and have embraced in their sanctifying influence so many youth of both sexes, these letters are given to the public with the hope, that under God, they may stimulate such youth to activity in the cause of Christ, and awaken a desire for those exalted spiritual attainments which it is their object to recommend.

The age in which we live demands a high standard of Christian character. Any thing which contributes to elevate it must be useful.

In presenting this little volume, the author has no apologies to offer. Not that he supposes it free from defects, or impervious to the shafts of criticism; but because, if it is calculated to be useful, apologies are unnecessary: if it is not, none, however labored or eloquent, can atone for so grand and radical a defect.

ESSAY

ON THE NATURE OF VITAL PIETY—ITS SAMENESS IN ALL AGES AND COUNTRIES—AND ITS VARIOUS ASPECTS IN DIFFERENT CIRCUMSTANCES.

TRUE religion not only enlightens the understanding, but rectifies the affections of the heart. All genuine feelings of piety are the effects of divine truth. The variety and intensity of these feelings depend on the different kinds of truth, and the various aspects in which the same truth is viewed; and also, on the distinctness and clearness with which it is presented to the mind. In a state of moral perfection, truth would uniformly produce all those emotions and affections which correspond with its nature, without the aid of any superadded influence. That these effects are not experienced by all who have the opportunity of knowing the truth, is a strong evidence of human depravity. In a state of moral depravity, the mind is incapable alike of perceiving and feeling the beauty and excellence of divine truth. The dead neither see nor feel, and man is by nature "dead in trespasses and sins." Hence, the necessity of the agency of the Holy Spirit to illuminate and regenerate the mind. The nature of divine agency, in every case, is inscrutable by mortals. "The wind bloweth where it listeth, and thou hearest the sound thereof, but canst not tell whence it cometh, or whither it goeth: so is every one that is born of the Spirit." We know, however, that the work of the Spirit, in the regeneration of the heart, is adapted to the rational nature of man. The thing to be accomplished is not the creation of some new faculty; it is a moral renovation; and all moral changes must be effected by understanding and choice. To put the soul, therefore, in that state in which it will rightly understand the truth, and cordially choose the highest good, is the end of regeneration. Truth, therefore, must be the means by which actual conversion to God takes place. "Being born again, not of corruptible seed, but of incorruptible, by the word of God, which liveth and abideth for ever." "Of his own will begat he us with the word of truth." "Sanctify them through thy truth: thy word is truth." Although piety in the heart is the effect of a divine operation, yet all its exercises take place agreeably to the common laws of our rational nature. The understanding is enlightened, the judgment is convinced, motives operate on the will, and conscience approves or disapproves. That the soul, in the exercises of piety, is under the renovating influences of the Holy Spirit, is not known by any consciousness which it has of these divine operations, but by the effects produced in a change of views and feelings; and this change is ascribed to God, because no other is able to produce it; and his word assures us that he is its author.

Now, as all men are endowed with the same natural susceptibilities, and as all Christians contemplate the same fundamental truths, the work of grace in the hearts of all must be substantially the same. All have, by the knowledge of the law, been convinced of sin; have been made to feel sorrow, shame, and compunction, upon the recollection of their transgressions; and to submit to the justice of the sentence of condemnation, which the law denounces against them. All have been made sensible of their own inability to save themselves, and under the influence of these humbling and penitent feelings, have been led to seek refuge in Jesus Christ, as the only hope of their souls. This plan of salvation appears glorious and suitable to all believers; so that they not only acquiesce in it, as the only method of salvation, but they are so well pleased with it, that they would not have another if they could. And in the acceptance of Christ as a complete Saviour, there is, in every case, some experience of joy and peace. Connected with the views which the true believer has of Christ as a Saviour, there is also a discovery, more or less clear, of the glory of the divine attributes, especially of those which are most conspicuously manifested in the cross of Christ. Holiness, justice, mercy, and truth shine, in the view of the sincere convert, with a lustre surpassing all other excellence; and God is venerated and loved for his own intrinsic excellence, as well as for the rich benefits bestowed upon us. But although these views may be distinguished, yet, in experience, they are not separated. The brightest discovery of divine excellence ever made, is God's love to our miserable race. The law of God is also viewed to be holy, just, and good, by every regenerated soul. The unrenewed heart never is, nor ever can be, reconciled to the law; "it is not subject to it, nor indeed can be:" but the "new man" delights in the law of God, and would not have one precept of it altered; and while it condemns all his feelings and works as imperfect, he approves of it still, and blames himself for his want of conformity to a rule so perfect.

Another thing in which the experience of all Christians is uniform, is, that they all are brought to a deliberate purpose to be on the Lord's side. On this point there is no hesitancy. Many are affected, and much agitated with religious impressions, and yet never come to a full decision to choose God and his service. They halt between two opinions, and have a divided mind. Such persons, however lively their feelings, are not yet truly converted: all true converts, after counting the cost, have settled this point for ever. And they can say with the Psalmist, "My heart is fixed, O God, my heart is fixed." They are, therefore, prepared now to comply with the terms of discipleship laid down by Christ himself. They are willing to "deny themselves, to take up their cross, and follow him; to forsake father and mother, wife and children, houses and lands, yea, also their own lives, for the sake of Him who gave himself for them."

Out of such views and feelings as have been described, arises an ardent hungering and thirsting after righteousness, an intense desire to know more of God, and to be admitted into closer union and more intimate communion with him. These habitual desires of the renewed soul find their proper expression in prayer, and lead to a patient and earnest waiting upon God in all the ordinances and means of his appointment. True piety, however, does not stop in mere desires, or in attendance on religious duties; it seeks to glorify God by action. The earnest inquiry of every soul inspired with the love of God, is, "Lord, what wouldst thou have me to do?" And wherever there is piety towards God, there will exist benevolence towards men. One of the most sensible emotions of the young convert is, "good-will to men;" a sincere desire for the welfare and eternal salvation of all, not even excepting its most inveterate enemies. And towards the children of God, there springs up a strong and tender affection. Such seem to be brethren indeed, because they are the brethren of Christ, and bear something of his image, in the humility, meekness, and benevolence of their charac ter. In short, genuine piety disposes and determines all who are its subjects, to obey and respect all the commandments of God, and to hate and avoid all sin, according to that declaration of David, "I esteem all thy precepts concerning all things to be right, and hate every false way."

In all the above-mentioned essential characteristics of piety, there is a sameness in the exercises of all true Christians. The same impression has been made on every renewed heart, and the only difference is, that it is imprinted more deeply on some than others; but still, the characters are identical; and therefore the evidences of a work of grace, contained in the holy Scriptures, are equally applicable to all persons who have been brought from darkness to light. There often is, moreover, a striking resemblance in those accompanying exercises and circumstances which are not essential. Awakened sinners are liable to the same erroneous conceptions, and usually fall into the same mistakes. They are all prone to think, that by reforming their lives, they can restore themselves to the favor of God. They commonly apply to the works of the law for relief, in the first instance; and when driven from this false refuge, by a clearer view of the spirituality and extent of the law, and the depth of their own depravity, they are apt to give up all for lost, and seriously to conclude that there is no hope in their case. They are all prone to misapprehend the nature of the Gospel: of its freeness they can at first form no conception; and therefore they think it necessary to come with some price in their hands—to obtain some kind of preparation or fitness, before they venture to come to Christ. And when it is clear that no moral fitness can be obtained until they apply to him, this legal spirit will lead the soul under conviction to think, that very deep and pungent distress will recommend it to Christ; and thus many are found seeking and praying for a more deep and alarming impression of their sin and danger. It is also very common to place undue dependence on particular means; especially on such as have been much blessed to others. Anxious souls are prone to think, that in reading some particular book, or in hearing some successful preacher, they will receive the grace of God which bringeth salvation; in which expectation they are generally disappointed, and are brought at last to feel that they are entirely dependent on sovereign grace; and that they can do nothing to obtain that grace. Before, they were like a drowning man catching at every thing which seemed to promise support; but now, they are like a man who feels that he has no support, but is actually sinking. Their cry, therefore, is now truly a cry for *mercy*. "God be merciful unto me a sinner." "Lord save, I perish." And it has often been proverbially said, "Man's extremity is God's opportunity," which is commonly realized by the soul cut off from all dependence on itself—the arm of the Lord is stretched forth to preserve it from sinking; the Saviour's voice of love and mercy is heard; light breaks in upon the soul, and it finds itself embraced in the arms of the Saviour; and so wonderful is the transition, that it can scarcely trust to its own experience.

This similarity of feelings in the experience of the pious has often been remarked, and has been justly considered a strong evidence of the divine origin of experimental religion: for how, otherwise, can this uniformity of the views and feelings of the pious, in all ages and countries, be accounted for? Enthusiasm assumes a thousand different shapes and hues, and is marked by no uniform characteristics; but scriptural piety is the same now as in the days of David and Asaph; the same as when Paul lived; the same as experienced by the pious fathers of the Christian church; the same as described by the Reformers, by the Puritans, and by the evangelical preachers and writers of the present day. When the

Gospel takes effect on any of the heathen, although it is certain that they never had the opportunity of learning any thing of this kind from others, yet we find them expressing the same feelings which are common to other Christians. Persons from different quarters of the globe, whose vernacular tongue is entirely different, yet speak the same language in religion. Members of churches, which hold no communion, and which, perhaps, view each other, when at a distance, as heretics, often, when brought together, recognize in one another dear brethren, who are of one mind in their religious experience.

The late eminently pious and learned theologian, the Rev. Dr. Livingston, related to me, not many years before his decease, a pleasant anecdote, which will serve to illustrate the point under consideration; and which I communicate to the public the more willingly, because I do not know that he has left any record of it behind him. While a student at the university of Utrecht, a number of pious persons from the town, and from among the students, were accustomed to meet for free conversation on experimental religion, and for prayer and praise, in a social capacity. On one of these occasions, when the similarity of the exercises of the pious, in all countries and ages, was the subject of conversation, it was remarked by one of the company, that there was then present a representative from each of the four quarters of the world. These were, Dr. Livingston from America, a young man from the Cape of Good Hope in Africa, another student from one of the Dutch possessions in the East Indies, and many natives of Europe of course. It was therefore proposed, that at the next meeting, the three young gentlemen first referred to, together with an eminently pious young nobleman of Holland, should each give a particular narrative of the rise and progress of the work of grace in his own soul. The proposal was universally acceptable; and accordingly, a narrative was heard from a native of each of the four quarters of the globe—of their views and feelings, of their trials and temptations, etc. The result was highly gratifying to all present; and I think Dr. Livingston said, that it was generally admitted by those present, that they had never before witnessed so interesting a scene. And since I have taken the liberty of mentioning the name of that venerable and distinguished theologian, I beg leave to add, that I have never seen a man who appeared to love vital piety more, or to understand its nature better.

But the identity of religious feeling which has been described above, is consistent with a great variety in many of the accompanying circumstances. Indeed, it seems probable, that each individual Christian has something distinctly characteristic in his own case; so that there exists at least as much difference in the peculiar features of the inner as of the outward man. The causes of this diversity are manifold: as first, the different degrees of grace received in the commencement of the divine life; secondly, the extent to which they have respectively run in sin, and the suddenness, or gradual nature of their change; thirdly, the degree of religious knowledge which is possessed; and finally, no small diversity arises from the various constitutional temperaments of different persons, which must have a powerful effect in giving complexion to the exercises of religion. To all which may be added, the manner in which persons under religious impressions are treated by their spiritual guides; and especially the manner in which the Gospel is preached to them.

It has been remarked by men of exact observation, that particular revivals of religion are often marked by something peculiar in the exercises, and in the spirit of those who are the subjects of them. In some revivals, convictions are more pungent and awful, or continued for a longer time, than in others; and the converts, in some revivals, appear to acquire a much deeper and more abiding impression of the reality and glory of divine things, and are evidently more under the constraining influence of the love of Christ, than is observable in other cases. These are subjects which deserve a careful investigation; and as revivals are increasing in frequency and extent in our churches, and as different modes of conducting them are in use, it is highly important, that some man of deep experience, and sober, impartial judgment, should make observations extensively, and communicate them to the religious public; which is, in many places, perplexed and distracted with the different methods of treatment recommended by different persons, and different parties. It may, however, be laid down as a sound maxim, that in proportion as the truth of God is clearly brought to view, and faithfully applied to the heart and conscience, the good effects will be manifest. Erroneous opinions, although mingled with the essential truths of the Gospel, will ever tend to mar the work of God. The good produced on any individual, or on a society, must not be judged of by the violence of the feelings excited, but by their character. Men may be consumed by a fiery zeal, and yet exhibit little of the meekness, humility, and sweet benevolence of Jesus. Great pretenders and high professors may be proud, arrogant, and censorious. When these are the effects, we may, without fear, declare, " that they know not what manner of spirit they are of." Any religion, however corrupt, may have its zealots; but true Christianity consists in the fruits of the Spirit, which are, " love, joy, peace, long-suffering, gentleness, goodness, faith, meekness, temperance."

Piety seems also to assume an aspect somewhat

different, in different ages and periods of the church. There is in human nature a strong tendency to run to extremes; and from one extreme, immediately to the opposite. And as the imperfections of our nature mingle with every thing which we touch, so piety itself is not exempt from the influence of the tendency above mentioned. In one age, or in one religious community, the leaning is to enthusiasm: in another, to superstition. At one time, religion is made to assume a severe and gloomy aspect; the conscience is morbidly scrupulous; things indifferent are viewed as sins; and human infirmities are magnified into crimes. At such times, all cheerfulness is proscribed; and the Christian whom nature prompts to smile, feels a check from the monitor within. This alloy of genuine piety is also often connected with bigotry and censoriousness. Now, when true religion is disfigured by such defects, it appears before the world to great disadvantage. Men of the world form their opinions of the nature of piety from what they observe in its professors; and from such an exhibition of it as we have described, they often take up prejudices which are never removed. There is, however, an opposite extreme, not less dangerous and injurious than this. When professors of religion conform to the world so far that no clear distinction can be observed between the Christian and the worldling. If the former error drives men away from religion, as a sour and miserable thing, this leads them to the opinion, that Christians are actuated by the same principles as they are; and therefore they conclude that no great change of their character is necessary. It is sometimes alleged by professors who thus accommodate themselves to the fashions and amusements of the world, that they hope by this means to render religion attractive, and thus gain over to piety those who neglect it; but this is a weak pretext, for such conformity always tends to confirm people in their carelessness. When they see professors at the theatre, or figuring in the ballroom, their conclusion either is, that there is no reality in vital piety, or that these professors act inconsistently.

The religious habits of some serious professors of religion are adapted to make a very unfavorable impression on the minds of sensible men. They assume a demure and sanctimonious air, and speak in an affected and drawling tone; often sighing, and lifting up their eyes, and giving audible utterance to their ejaculations. Now, these persons may be, and I doubt not, often are, truly pious; but the impression made on most minds, by this affectation of religious solemnity, is, that they are hypocrites, who aim at being thought uncommonly devout. It appears to me, that religion never appears so lovely, as when she wears the dress of perfect simplicity. We ought not, indeed, to be ashamed of our religion before the world; but it behooves us to be very careful, not to give to others an unfavorable opinion of serious piety. The rule is, "Let your light *so* shine, that others seeing your good works, may glorify your Father who is in heaven." "Let not your good be evil spoken of."

But the aspect and character of the piety of one age may differ from that of another, more from the peculiar circumstances in which Christians are placed, than from the prevalence of erroneous views or incorrect habits. In one age, vital piety seeks retirement, and runs in hidden channels. At such a time, the attention of Christians is turned chiefly on themselves. Much time is devoted to devotional exercises; often whole days. The secret recesses of the heart are explored with diligence and rigor; indwelling sin is detected in its multiform appearances, and is mortified with invincible resolution; the various means of personal growth in grace are studied, and used with persevering assiduity; and much useful knowledge of the nature of the spiritual life in the soul is acquired. But while vital piety is thus carefully cultivated, and the attention is earnestly turned to the exercises of the heart, there may be very little display of active, enlarged benevolence; there may be few vigorous efforts made to meliorate the condition of the multitudes perishing in sin. Under the influence of these defective views of the nature of religion, many pious persons, in the early ages of Christianity, withdrew entirely from the world, and lived in the wilderness; which mistake occasioned innumerable evils to the church, the effects of which are not yet obliterated.

The spirit of piety among the Reformers seems to have been pure and vigorous, but not as expansive as it might have been. They seem scarcely to have thought of the hundreds of millions of heathen in the world; and of course, made no efforts to extend the knowledge of salvation to them. Indeed, they were so much occupied at home, in contending for the faith against the Romanists, that they had little time left for benevolent enterprises at a distance; but if that zeal which was worse than wasted in controversy with one another, had been directed to the conversion of the heathen, their usefulness would have been far greater than it was.

The Puritans, also, although profoundly acquainted with experimental religion, seemed to have confined their attention too exclusively to themselves. Their ministers were, it is true, silenced, and driven into corners and into exile, by an ungrateful and tyrannical government; but it seems wonderful to us, that when prevented from preaching the Gospel to their own countrymen, they did not turn to the gentiles. But the era of missions had not yet arrived, and probably they had but small opportunity, in their persecuted state, of uniting their counsels, or combining their energies in schemes of distant benevolence. One thing, however, is now manifest, that the providence of God overruled the retirement and leisure of those godly ministers who were ejected from their charges, so as to render their labors more useful to the church than if they had been permitted to spend their lives in preaching the Gospel; for, when deprived of the liberty of employing their tongues, they betook themselves to their pens, and they have left to the church such a body of practical and casuistical theology, as all ages, before or since, cannot equal. I have no doubt, that such men as Owen, Baxter, Flavel, Bunyan, Goodwin, Manton, Howe, and Bates, have effected much more good by their practical writings, than they could possibly have done by their preaching, supposing them to have been ever so successful.

But our lot is cast in a different age, and in a different state of the church. After a long slumber, the attention of Christians has been aroused to consider the perishing condition of the heathen. We live in a period when great designs are entertained, and plans formed for the conversion of the whole world; when one benevolent enterprise or institution follows another in rapid succession, until the Christian community begins to exhibit an entirely new aspect from what it did within our own remembrance. Christians have begun to feel, that by a combination of effort, they have power to accomplish much. The public attention is kept awake by the frequent recurrence of public meetings of an interesting kind, and by that more potent engine, the wide circulation of religious PERIODICALS, by which, interesting intelligence is conveyed to almost every corner of our extensive country. The duty of Christians to be active, is now inculcated in almost every form; Tracts are multiplied; the Scriptures are circulated; the young and ignorant are instructed by new methods; and many are found running to and fro to promote the propagation of evangelical truth. Revivals of religion, also, are exerting a mighty influence on the church. The number of serious Christians is vastly increased; and many youth are brought forward to a course of preparation for the gospel ministry. A spirit of liberality also is witnessed, unknown to our fathers; and the duty of consecrating to the Lord a reasonable proportion of all their increase, is beginning to be extensively felt among serious Christians. And such is the spirit of enterprise, that no undertaking appears too arduous, which has for its object the advancement of the Redeemer's kingdom: and such is the favor of heaven towards benevolent enterprises in our day, that scarcely one has failed of accomplishing some good; and although the schemes of benevolence are so various and so multiplied, yet there has occurred no sensible interference of one with another. As they all aim at the same object, so they are all viewed as parts of the same great system of operations. Now, in all these favorable appearances and benevolent exertions, every pious heart must and will rejoice.

But is there no danger, that many who feel interested in the operations of the day, and contribute to their advancement, should be mistaken as to their true spiritual condition? When a powerful current takes a set, many will be carried along with it, whichever way it may run. And is there no danger that Christians themselves, while they seem to flourish in external profession, zeal, and activity, may be decaying at the root, for want of sufficient attention to their own hearts, and to the duties of the closet? There is, indeed, much reason to fear that many professors now exist, who confine their religion too much to those external acts which may be performed from motives no higher than those which operate on unrenewed men. The danger now is, that the religion of the heart will be neglected, and that many will feel well satisfied with themselves, on account of their activity and zeal, who are yet strangers to a work of grace. This being the point on which Christians of the present day are liable to err, it is a matter of congratulation, that some writers seem disposed to turn the attention of the Christian public to the importance of diligence and punctuality in performing the duties of the closet. The following letters are well calculated to produce this effect. They were forwarded to me by an esteemed young clergyman, who is settled as a pastor in a distant and retired village. They were addressed, as the author has stated in his preface, to a young lady of highly respectable connections, upon the occasion of her making a public profession of religion. The father of this young lady, who is distinguished for his benevolence and evangelical piety, was unwilling that the pious and judicious counsels, and affectionate exhortations which they contain, should be limited to an individual, since they are so well adapted to be useful to Christians generally, and especially to the young, placed in circumstances similar to those of the person to whom they were originally addressed. A request was therefore made for their publication. The author, through modesty, has withheld his name, but has requested me to introduce them to the public with some preliminary essay of my own; with which request I have here complied, believing that the letters of my young friend are seasonable, judicious, and pious, and that as they are written in an ornate and animated style, they will be extensively perused by the young.

A. ALEXANDER.

PRINCETON, N. J.

ADVICE
TO
A YOUNG CHRISTIAN

LETTER I.

FORMING AN ELEVATED CHRISTIAN CHARACTER.

Dear Young Friend—You are very young to profess the high character of a Christian; but your youth, while it serves as a caution, should not operate as a discouragement. Many a person of fewer years, and with less advantages, has not only given satisfactory evidence of conversion, but proved, in subsequent life, to be of that number whose "path shineth more and more, unto the perfect day."

It becomes you, however, to look narrowly into the evidences of such a change. A mistake here will prove fatal. The word of God and prayer are the great means, which, if faithfully applied, will in due time develope your true moral character. If you have been deceived, if yet in your sins, these duties will ere long become irksome, and be loosely performed or utterly neglected. If you have been regenerated, you will not only persevere in these duties, but will find that they elicit more and more of your interest, until you arrive at a well-grounded hope of eternal felicity.

Taking for granted that you do not make this profession on slight grounds, nor with inadequate or erroneous views, my object, in a few letters which I shall address to you, will be to urge you to the formation of an elevated Christian character. You profess to have taken the first step in the strait and narrow way; but recollect, it is *only* the first step. The concentrated gaze of many eyes is upon you. Some would exult in your downfall—others rejoice in your advancement. Invisible and wicked spirits will tempt you to ruin. Good and guardian angels will watch around your steps, and rejoice in your victories. To sustain *yourself* you have already been convinced is impossible. If you are regenerated, you are not perfectly sanctified; nor *will* you be until death shall be swallowed up in victory. But as Paul could do all things, by the strength of his Master, so can the weakest believer; and you must ever feel that the same grace which brought you "out of nature's darkness," must enable you to overcome your enemies, and "persevere unto the end."

As I have touched upon this point, I am forcibly reminded of the beautiful dream of the Rev. John

CHRISTIAN CHARACTER. 29

Newton, while lying at anchor in the harbor of Venice, and within sight of a part of the Alps. For the particulars I refer you to his volumes. The substance is as follows.

The anxiety of mind which he endured in his waking hours, seemed to give a coloring to his night-vision. He felt himself in great perplexity and horror. While musing on the wretchedness of his condition, there appeared suddenly a celestial figure, who presented to him a ring, which she said, if preserved with care, would, on every difficult occasion, resolve his doubts, and extricate him from trouble. He was overjoyed at the reception of it. All his fears seemed to subside, and a heavenly serenity to succeed. While in this tranquil and happy frame of mind, another personage, of less inviting aspect, made his appearance, and, after many flattering words and artful insinuations, prevailed on him to part with the ring. He deliberately dropped it over the side of the vessel, and it sunk to the bottom. The flames, in an awful manner, immediately burst from the mountain, and he seemed threatened with instant destruction. At this moment of horror, his celestial friend again appeared, and, with a frown of mingled love and reproof, upbraided him for listening to the voice of the tempter. She then descended into the water, and soon returned bearing the ring, and thus addressed him: "As thou art unable to keep this token, I will preserve it for thee, and it shall be secure for ever."

I have only given you from memory an outline of this beautiful vision. The interpretation which the author put upon it is full of spiritual instruction. If left for one moment to our own strength, how soon do we abandon the "ring," even at the first suggestion of the tempter. Then the soul is affrighted and dismayed. But Jesus, our guardian, is able to restore the "ring," and lest we should lose it, he, in condescension to our infirmities, deigns to keep it. "I will never leave thee, nor forsake thee," is his language. Thus, my dear young friend, intrust the "ring" to Him who alone is able to preserve it. When the tempter comes, whether in the artful guise of what the world calls innocent pleasure, or the bold assaults of blasphemy and despair, look upwards to Him who is charged with the care of all that is precious to the soul. Wait not until you are overwhelmed by the consciousness of contracted guilt, but flee—oh, flee, as for your life, to Jesus. You cannot trust him too confidently. He will permit you to sit even at his feet. There is honor, there is safety, there is happiness.

I congratulate you on the favorable circumstances in which you are placed for the formation of Christian character. The work of divine grace in which you profess to be a participant, is, I understand, still in progress. Doubtless you find some congenial spirits, with whom you can mingle feelings, unite in mutual prayer, and converse on the sweetest of all topics, the love of your Lord and Master. Let it be a principle with you, to select as your companions the most heavenly-minded of your sex. If such can be found in the higher walks of life, very well; be they your bosom friends: but, alas, how seldom, in the higher circles, does religion, in its native simplicity and purity, appear. You must seek it, I apprenend, in the low vale of obscurity, and often amid the homely attire of honest poverty. If you have the spirit of Christ, you will love his image, though arrayed in an humble garb. I know it has ever been the design of your parents to make you estimate character, not by riches, nor fashionable appearance, but by intrinsic moral worth; and I am persuaded that you must now feel, that if Providence has given you advantages of wealth and education above the plainest rustic, it is a ground of humility, inasmuch as it lays you under the greater obligations. Where "much is given"—oh, never forget it—"much will be required." On this principle, are you not bound to be humble, benevolent, condescending?

In closing this letter, I must say to you as I lately said to a youth in my congregation, who is about making a public profession of her faith in Christ, "I hope you will not be satisfied with being half a

Christian." So, my young friend, I would exhort you to aim high. It is a day to elevate the standard of piety. We want more Newels, and Huntingtons, and Ramsays, and Smelts. These were devoted souls. It was not half-way work with them. Religion was "all in all." For this they lived, they suffered, and, supported by its consolations, they died. They have left a bright track for you to follow. Tread closely in their steps; and then, though you share in their sufferings, you shall also inherit, with them, the "crown of glory."

LETTER II.

TEMPTATIONS.

Among the first temptations which you will probably experience, will be an effort, on the part of your spiritual enemies, to seduce you back to the pleasures of the world. Sometimes it will be a direct and powerful attack. The ways of religion will be represented as difficult, whilst those of worldly pleasure will be strewed with flowers. "What," the tempter will exclaim, "shall one so young, so susceptible of enjoyment from all the varied delights of sense—one who has it in her power to command almost any imaginable happiness—shall she put on the grave aspect of piety, and thus debar herself from every innocent pleasure? Look abroad, see thy young companions, how their hearts beat with rapture, as they float amid the circles of beauty and of fashion. Why shouldst thou become a sober religionist, when thou art ripening for so much bliss? In such false and flattering colors will the tempter array the world. Knowing that vanity is one of the strongest principles of our depraved nature, he will constantly, and often successfully, appeal to it. His flatteries will respect your person, your accomplishments, your fortune. He will suggest, that with such advantages the world must pay you homage, and become a sort of perpetual paradise.

Had you, my young friend, been one of pleasure's gay votaries, as *I* have been, he could not, and probably he would not, thus address you. I could say, from experience, Thou seducing spirit, what thou sayest is false. Have I not mingled in the festival? Have I not courted pleasure in the brilliant assembly and the crowded theatre, where beauty and wealth have poured around their shining and fascinating attractions? And what did I ever gain? A momentary rapture, I admit; an exhilaration of spirits, and a temporary oblivion of my cares. But this was all. And even these transitory joys were not unalloyed. Jealousy, and envy, and hatred, and disappointment, would occasionally let fall the bitter drop, as the cup was passing to the lip; and satiety, disgust, and self-loathing would succeed. But conscience was more powerful than all. What restless hours of wakeful solicitude, what anticipated wrath, what vain resolutions, what unavailing regrets! And shall the tempter tell me that the pleasures of the world are worthy to be preferred to the calm delight of communion with God, and the high enjoyments of religion? "He was a liar from the beginning;" and when, my young Christian friend, he assaults you with such suggestions, or when, through his emissaries in human form, he would seduce you from your allegiance, recollect his character, resist his suggestions—and, according to the promise, "he will flee from you."

But it is far more probable, that his insinuations will be almost imperceptible. A direct and powerful attack may throw a Christian on his face, and overwhelm him with agony; but Judah's lion shall appear, and affright the bold adversary. It is when your spiritual enemies are making a gradual advance on your purity and devotedness, that they are most to be dreaded, as most likely to be successful. Now, you are, I trust, conscientious in the discharge of the duty of private devotion. You love to retire from human observation, to commune with God. I would fain believe, that you are never so happy as when thus engaged; that you have a consecrated spot, which you call your Bethel, where the soul daily drinks in the waters of life.

Happy, dear youth, happy will you be, if that Bethel is always thus attractive and interesting. But the great danger is, that it will be neglected, and perhaps forsaken. You are ready to exclaim, "Impossible; I shall never cease to pray. I could sooner dispense with my daily food, than forego the privileges of a throne of grace." This is the language of sincerity, I doubt not. You verily think so; but how little do you know the temptations which surround you, and the deceitfulness of your own heart? You have much to fear.

When called myself from nature's darkness, and made, as I hope, to taste the sweetness of redeeming love, I was of the same opinion. I had waked up in a new world. 'Twas as if the Creator had formed a new being, akin to the happy spirits in heaven, and dropped him on the earth in the spring-time of nature's magnificence and beauty. The foliage seemed greener and fresher than ever. The dew-drops glittered more brilliantly; the sky looked purer; and every thing seemed to shine and wave in silent but emphatic praise of God their Creator. My soul beat in happy unison with these silent worshippers, and methought I could never cease to sing and pray. My very being seemed to consist in it. But has it been so ever since? Oh, ye hours of anguish, ye days of sensuality, ambition, and folly; ye can say how guilty, how careless, how ungrateful I have been. Little did I then dream of loving and serving the world. I thought I could have spent an eternity of happiness on some lonely rock in the ocean, if God were with me there. I thought my soul would never forsake him, nor my voice ever be silent in his praise. But I knew not my own heart, nor the power of the world's allurements.

Now do not suppose, that because I and others have been tempted to backslide, and have yielded to the temptation, you must necessarily follow our disgraceful defection. I hope you never will. If you are a child of God, you need not. You may go "from strength to strength." You may accomplish victory after victory. God grant that you may.

But should you, by mournful experience, have to look upon yourself as a backslider, you will remember this warning, and wish you had heeded it. Like the prodigal, you will be in spiritual beggary. I know of no condition, except that of hardened impenitence, more pitiable than the condition of a backslider. Conscience is too quick to allow him to enjoy the world; and religion is too much neglected to yield him the smallest comfort. He lives in disquietude and anguish, until he repents, and finds anew the favor of his God.

LETTER III.

DANGER OF BACKSLIDING.

In my last, I touched upon the subject of temptation. I am constrained to add a few words more on the same subject. It has been too common for those who have betrayed their Lord by a disgraceful return to the world, to predict the same defection in others. Hence, you often hear professors of religion address the youthful convert in such language as the following: "Your present ardor is no proof that it will continue; now you are all joy, all devotion; by and by the scene will be changed. I once felt as you now feel; perhaps I enjoyed more ecstatic pleasure; but I soon lost the glow of my first love, and so will you. A few years will cool you down, and show you that such engagedness cannot always last."

When I hear such language addressed to the young Christian, I am indignant. It is not necessarily true; my young friend, it is not true. The Bible, which is the only "lamp to our path," gives no warrant for such a prediction. True, it represents the cases of many who at first bade fair, but subsequently apostatized. It records the cases of such, as a flaming beacon, to warn those who should come after them. But does it not represent the path of the just, as "the shining light, which shineth more and more unto the perfect day?" Does it not say, that he who hath clean hands, shall grow "stronger and stronger?" Does it not urge us to "grow in grace," to "forget the things which are behind," and "reach towards those which are before?" to make Christ our mark and press towards it, with all the energy of an Olympic racer, struggling in competition for the goal?

Now, I warn you not to listen to such cold predictions. They who make them from their own experience, may have been hypocrites. They may have felt something, which they called spiritual joy; but perhaps it was "Satan transformed into an angel of light:" perhaps it was the workings of their own imaginations, and not the legitimate fruits of the Spirit. Let them take heed to themselves, lest they have been deceived; and not allure others on, in their down-hill course, by their disgraceful example. But suppose them to have been Christians—and I allow that a Christian may grow cold, and backslide in the service of God—is such language warranted by the word of God? Is it likely to urge forward the young convert in the path of holiness? Is it likely to raise the standard of piety in the souls of others? No; far from it. Young converts are prone to copy those who are older and more experienced. If they are persuaded that it is consistent with the existence of piety to grow cold in feeling, they will probably yield to the seductions of the world, and the temptations of Satan. They will not press forward; they will recede. They will take the cold, dead level of their predecessors.

But, my young friend, be you warned by this, not to listen to such language for a moment; nor to suppose it must be true in your case. I do assure you, your Bible holds a different language. As you value your comfort, your peace of mind, your immortal hopes, your character as a Christian, your influence as a follower of the Lamb, press forward. Strive every day to make some new attainments in knowledge and holiness. You are engaged in a conflict. You have put on the armor of God; and put it off for a moment you must not. Your enemies are numerous, vigilant, and powerful. You must contend every day: nor must you think of rest or relaxation. When death shall unbind for you the gospel armor, and you hear the dark waves of Jordan lashing these mortal shores, then, and not till then, will your struggles be ended, and your victory complete. You have counted the cost; do not shrink at the cross. Christ will be with you. Christ will support you. Under his banner you contend. His arm will shield you, and his grace bring you off more than conqueror.

I have digressed a little from the point at which I aimed. I wished to caution you particularly, concerning the first step in a backward course. The

BACKSLIDING. 41

first step in the retreat is an important one. It is needful, therefore, to say, that generally, that step commences at the closet. Prayer is the strong hold to which the young Christian generally resorts. In doubts and difficulties, a throne of grace is his refuge. If the "devouring lion" roar, thither the lamb will flee, and house itself in the bosom of its shepherd. If the world entice, and for a moment soil his purity, thither he repairs, and the stain is washed out in the blood of Jesus. If the path of duty be not obvious, if perplexity attend his course, at a throne of grace there is light and direction. Hence, it will be an important advantage to your enemies, if they can draw you from this palladium, this strong tower of defence. Keep alive, then, I beseech you, to the first symptom of declension in prayer. Prayer is a difficult, often an arduous work; but it is the life and soul of a Christian. It is not only his incumbent duty, but his most precious privilege.

Now, it will be the aim of the tempter, to withdraw you from being "instant in prayer." He knows what a powerful weapon it is; and therefore he will endeavor to wrest it out of your hands. He will represent it as an irksome duty. He will suggest that fewer and shorter prayers will answer. He will interpose obstacles between you and your closet. He will divert your attention while there, and then taunt you with your coldness and your folly. He will say that your prayers are hypocritical—insincere—an abomination to God. He will suggest, that now you are not in a good frame—advise you to put it off until you feel in a better. Thus will he try every art, and use every machination to draw you from this refuge of your soul. But, "Get thee behind me, Satan," must be your reply to all such suggestions. You must cling closer to the "horns of the altar." You must "bind the sacrifice with cords," if you cannot keep it there. You must give yourself to prayer, and to the word of God. Like the vestals, you **must** live at the altar.

LETTER IV.

PRAYER.

I FEEL constrained, my young friend, to add something more on the subject of PRAYER. This duty, in my view, is of such importance as to warrant a few more remarks; although I do not intend enlarging on a subject upon which so much, and such excellent things have been written.

You were taught by your pious parents, to utter a form of prayer, as soon as your infant mind could comprehend, and your infant tongue enunciate a sentence. In looking back upon these juvenile devotions, you doubtless see wherein they were deficient. Your ideas of the Being to whom they were addressed, were confused and inadequate. You could not then comprehend the necessity of a Mediator; for as yet you had not discovered the evil of sin, and the wrath of God, as revealed against it. You had too deep a sense of obligation, to neglect prayer entirely; but of the real nature and efficacy of prayer, you had little conception. To your mind, prayer was a form of words to be repeated at stated intervals. When thus repeated, the obligation was discharged. This was probably all you knew about prayer.

But shall parents omit to inculcate this duty on their children, because they cannot comprehend the nature of it? Certainly not. How can they tell but that, when they have taught the little prattler to compose himself to rest with his familiar and simple petitions, the Spirit of God may enlighten the child into the spiritual import of his prayer, and make it a means of leading him to more enlarged petitions, offered up "in spirit and in truth?" No person can estimate the advantages of early imbuing the youthful mind with a sense of its obligations to God. Such instructions should commence with the first dawn of intellect; and sure I am, that in subsequent life, the subject of them will generally be the better and the happier.

To illustrate this, I will recur again to my own case. I was taught by one of the best of mothers, never to close my eyes without repeating my prayers. This I conscientiously adhered to, until about thirteen or fourteen years of age, when I began gradually to omit them. Whether I felt that they were too childish, or whether, as is most probable, my conscience was becoming seared in the down-hill course of iniquity, I cannot now remember. But at all events, my prayers were no longer offered; and I went to sleep and rose up like a brute With the omission of these prayers commenced a retrograde movement in morals, until I hung over the abyss of ruin, ripe for the judgments of God. And what do you suppose occurred first to rouse me from the fatal slumbers of death? As I was retiring one night, the recollection of my former punctilious attention to prayer rushed upon my mind. I paused. "What," said I to myself, "am I going to lie down without one thought of God, or offering one prayer for the safety of my soul? Did I not once repeat my prayers; and at a time too when I was far less guilty than now? Why have I omitted them so long? Suppose I should die this night, where then would my soul be?" With such reflections I became impressed; and although I did not kneel that night, yet in a recumbent posture I began again to repeat my juvenile devotions. I was nearly seventeen years of age when I resumed them. I had almost forgotten them. A few days and nights rolled away, and convictions grew heavier on my soul. I thought a repetition of these forms was not enough. My soul began to sink in the deep waters; and a few more days brought me on my knees at the bedside, with the prayer of the publican, "God be merciful to me a sinner."

Thus, my young friend, were my mother's early instructions among the means, under God, of rescuing me from ruin, temporal and eternal. Thus it is evident, that the sooner children are taught to pray, the better; and no assiduity can be too great to impress on them the obligation and the necessity of prayer.

Still, I believe that the Christian only prays the acceptable prayer. Until the Spirit of God convince of sin, the soul will not see its odiousness, nor pray for its removal. The danger to which it is exposed here and hereafter, it may see; and it may deprecate the punishment to which it is subjected; but it is only when the soul is renewed in the image of God, that "sin appears exceeding sinful," and that the effectual fervent prayer for sanctification is offered.

If you are a Christian, my young friend, the throne of grace is yours. Your Father is seated on it. Your Saviour has sprinkled it with his blood. The Holy Spirit draws you sweetly to kneel before it; and the promise, when there, is, "Open your mouth wide, and I will fill it." What an honor thus to approach the King of kings. Were we to have audience with an earthly monarch, we should deem it an era in our history, and boast of it through life. But you, and I, and others, may have audience with the King of the universe. Nay, we have liberty to approach him at any time, and under all circumstances. Have we wants, he can supply them. Are we in trouble, he can extricate us. Do afflictions press our souls, he can mitigate and remove them. Does sin pollute our joys, with him is the fountain of cleansing. Does Satan vex our souls, he invites us to his arms as our refuge. All relief and every blessing is with God.

There is nothing which so elevates a character, and especially a female character, as deep and intimate communion with God. She seems then to be allied to angelic natures. A sort of mellow radiance is poured into her character, as if some particles of heaven's glory had been let fall upon her. She moves in a higher sphere than the generality of her sex. She is another being than those idle, sickly daughters of pleasure, who waste their lives in dreaming fanciful visions of happiness, sporting a while amid life's tumultuous joys, and then sinking unblessed into a wretched eternity. She converses with God. At a throne of grace she acquires a benevolence, a dignity, a humility, which throw around her an attractive lustre, put sweetness into every action and expression, make her contented in every condition of life, patient under every affliction, faithful in the discharge of every duty, and which even grace her dying hours, and make her "death-bed privileged beyond the common walks of life."

LETTER V.

PRAYER—CONTINUED.

There are three inquiries, my young friend, respecting prayer, which every conscientious Christian will be likely to institute. How ought I to pray, when, or at what times, and for what things? These are important inquiries. A full and satisfactory answer I feel myself unable to give. I shall, in my desultory way, barely touch upon each.

Those who worship God, are bound to "worship him in spirit and in truth." In spirit, as opposed to the mere external ceremonies. The Jews and the Samaritans, at the time our Lord uttered the prediction just alluded to, were reposing an unfounded confidence in the mere forms and ceremonies of their religion; while, in the emphatic language of inspiration, their "hearts were far from God."

We must pray, then, with the spirit. The heart must be in the work, or it will be insincere and ineffectual. The Quakers, you know, reject all external forms. They may be regarded as on one extreme. The Jews and Catholics, having a multitude of forms, are on the other. I would not insinuate, that among Quakers and Catholics, there are no sincere worshippers; far from it. I believe there are many devout

Christians among both. I am persuaded, for my own part, that some attention to form and circumstance is an important auxiliary to us poor weak mortals, in our attempts to worship God. In my own experience, I have found the benefit of it. For example, when I have a particular room allotted to my devotions—a certain place in that room, where I am accustomed to kneel—a degree of obscurity shed over the place by the exclusion of too great a glare of light; all these circumstances are a help to me, by the power of mental association. There is nature in this: and God permits us to have recourse to every lawful auxiliary in worshipping him. The great point is, to worship " in spirit and in truth."

True worship is distinguished from false, inasmuch as the one is scriptural, but the other is not. A tru. worshipper views the character of God as it is de lineated in the Bible. The omniscience, omnipresence, holiness, justice, goodness, and truth of God, are attributes of delightful contemplation; and centering in one eternal, unchangeable, and incomprehensible Spirit, they excite his reverence, his confidence, his humility, and his love. He looks into his Bible to learn the character of God; and, as there found, worships him in spirit and in truth.

But can a guilty creature, who has violated every obligation he is under to his Creator, approach him without the intervention of a Mediator? I bring this question home to myself, and inquire, would I dare, as a suppliant, to approach my God and my Creator in all my uncovered, aggravated guilt? This, my young friend, is the hinge of salvation. The Socinian will tell me, Certainly you may. But my own conscience would give a different verdict. I see naught in my life but sin—sin of the most aggravated kind: I repeat these sins, and confess them; and again repeat them. Now I say, Is God holy? Is he opposed to sin? Then must I fall under his wrath and curse. Then how can I expect to escape his indignation? He is merciful, says the Socinian. True, he *is* merciful; but is not that mercy exercised in a peculiar way? Is it indiscriminate, unconditional mercy? Must not something be done to show God's abhorrence of my sins? Must not some sacrifice be made? Now I am brought to the delightful, soul-cheering feature of the Gospel: "God in *Christ*, reconciling the world unto himself, not imputing their trespasses unto them." "He so loved the world, that he gave his only begotten Son, that whosoever believeth in him, should not perish, but have everlasting life." "He was wounded for our transgressions." On this foundation my soul finds firm footing, and I rest secure in the promise of eternal life. Whosoever cometh unto the Father, therefore, must come through Christ; and so coming, shall not be cast out.

All acceptable prayer is rendered so by the merits and intercession of the divine Saviour. He is our merciful and faithful High-priest. His own blood was shed for the remission of our sins : and the apostle says, "If any man sin, we have an advocate with the Father, Jesus Christ the righteous." When you pray, therefore, never lose sight of the Mediator. "His name is like ointment poured forth." The sinner's friend, he pleads the sinner's cause. He knows your infirmities, your temptations, and your trials, and is ever ready to afford you relief.

The doctrine of the Trinity is, I know, offensive to many who are governed more by carnal reason than by Scripture ; but to me, if I am not deceived, it is one of the most comforting, cheering, and elevating truths of the Bible. I see the persons of the Godhead harmoniously engaged in my deliverance. In prayer, the Spirit seems to lift my lagging affections, and to carry them upwards, pouring light into the dark chambers of the mind. Jesus the Mediator pleads my cause, even when my own tongue is dumb with grief, and my soul overwhelmed with conscious guilt. Then the throne of grace is precious, and the soul is replenished as with marrow and fatness.

I pity those whose scepticism has blotted out the glory of our Immanuel. Their religion is cold. It warms not the heart ; it pacifies not the conscience ; it prompts to few acts of self-denial ; it almost obliterates the line between the righteous and the wicked; and it makes retribution a farce. After all, it is only a substitute, and a very poor one, for the glorious Gospel of the Son of God.

Having been inadvertently led, by the subject, to these remarks, I must now return. In prayer we must be earnest—we must be sincere—we must have faith in the promises. The "fervent prayer availeth much." "Jacob wrestled;" what a strong expression. Jesus, in prayer, sweat drops of blood. Paul prayed with tears. Hannah wept at the altar. All these examples, and numerous others, such as the widow pleading with the unjust judge, show the necessity of earnestness in prayer. This, I know, is often difficult. You will come to the mercy-seat with a cold heart and wandering thoughts; and how, at such times, can you be fervent? "The Spirit helpeth our infirmities," is the only reply I can offer. And this is sufficient. In such a frame of mind there is the greater need of earnestness. Tarry not until your thoughts take a more elevated and spiritual tone. I have always found that the best way of proceeding in such a case, was to apply immediately to a throne of grace. There wrestle; renew the supplication, and still renew it; until, as is often the case, the fire of heaven descends, and the sacrifice is enkindled. The Lord give you the spirit and the success of the patriarch Jacob.

LETTER VI.

SINCERITY IN PRAYER.

SINCERITY, my dear young friend, is an essential ingredient in prayer. Without it, no prayer can be acceptable. Indeed, if we are insincere, we cannot be said to pray. A mere form of words is not prayer.

Prayer is the desire of the heart for something which we judge to be necessary or beneficial. It implies a knowledge of our wants, and an urgent wish to have them supplied. If, therefore, the heart be roving after one object, while the lips are employed in asking for another, we are insincere and unacceptable worshippers. Such conduct is an insult to our Creator—a game of deception on ourselves. Such were the petitions at which God, in old times, declared himself indignant; when his professing people drew "nigh unto him with their mouth, and honored him with their lips, while their heart was far from him." Such was the religion of the scribes and Pharisees; fair and beautiful without, but within all rottenness and corruption.

Reflect a moment ere you bend the knee at the throne of grace. I am not now about to approach an earthly monarch, who, though surrounded with the pomp and circumstance of royalty, is but a worm of the dust like myself; but I am to have audience with the King of kings—the Lord of the whole earth. I am about to come into the presence, and to utter the name of Him at whose fiat all creation sprang into existence. Were I in the presence of a finite being, I might, perhaps, conceal my feelings under a form of words. I might utter one thing and mean another. But can I thus practise deception with God? Are not all things "naked, and opened unto the eyes of Him with whom we have to do?" Does not he search the hearts of the children of men? Will he be satisfied with any thing but "truth in the inward parts?" "If I regard iniquity in my heart," says the sweet singer of Israel, "the Lord will not hear me." And again, in his bold and beautiful interrogatories, "He that formed the eye, shall he not see? He that created the ear, shall he not hear?"

Let such be your meditation when you are about to kneel at the throne of grace. Not that I would array the character of God in terrors to your mind, or send you to tremble like a slave at his feet. No, he is a God of love, of compassion, of long forbearance; more beneficent and tender than the kindest earthly parent. You may go to him, and you must so go, in the confiding simplicity of a child and a favorite. When you take to him the name of **Christ** your Mediator, you take, so to speak, a passport into his very bosom. You may unburden your whole heart; tell him things which you could confide to no mortal ear; make confession of sins which you dare only whisper in your closet; and in the ingenuous frankness of faith and penitence, humbly cast yourself on his all-supporting arm. He is your covenant God; and, when alone with him, you may indulge even a holy familiarity.

Reflect on your own character, as well as on that of the Being whom you address: the thought of both will humble you in the dust, and prepare you, in your approach to the mercy-seat, to appreciate the all-glorious, divine, and compassionate Mediator. Be careful to inquire into your wants. Say within yourself, Why have I now retired? What errand have I at the throne; what sins to confess, what mercies to acknowledge, what wants to be supplied? For whom, besides myself, should I pray? What temptations appear to be most formidable? Let me not cover one sin, nor keep back one confession. Let me not ask for holiness, if I would retain a single lust; if I am not resolved to crucify all. Let me not ask for a revival of religion, if I do not secretly and sincerely wish for it. "Search me, O God, and know my heart, and see if there be any wicked way in me, and lead me in the way everlasting," should ever be your wish and your petition. Let your sincerity be such that you can ever thus appeal to the heart-searching God. Nothing is so well calculated to foster the spirit of devotion, as to be enabled to say with Peter, "thou knowest;" to make the familiar appeal, although I cannot, by reason of infirmity, express the number and aggravation of my sins, yet, oh Lord, "thou knowest" I lament them, and sincerely desire their removal; although my words fail in expressing my gratitude, yet "thou knowest" my heart is full; although I cannot give expression to my feelings in behalf of Zion, yet "thou knowest" I love her prosperity, and earnestly desire her increase and glory. "Thou knowest" is a sweet expression in the ears of a prayer-hearing God. It gives the soul a confidence and an earnestness, when pleading for itself or for others.

You will find, my young friend, strong temptations to be superficial and hurried in your prayers. Your enemies will suggest some engagements which will preclude or cut short your supplications. They will insinuate, that all this meditation is unnecessary. If in these attacks they prevail, you will immediately perceive an insincerity in your prayers. You will find yourself, at times, wishing the prayer was over; and uttering it, rather as a sedative to conscience, than as the supreme delight of your soul. You will then, indeed, come like a slave to the altar; and, having performed to conscience, as to an unrelenting tyrant, the accustomed task, you will be glad of a speedy relief. You may even find yourself, at times, uttering words and forms, of the meaning of which, while your heart is wandering on forbidden objects, you are totally unconscious. This is sinful in the extreme.

May you never arrive at this melancholy pitch of insult, and of mockery.

Yield not, dear young friend, to the power of the tempter. Give him no advantage over you; dispute every inch of ground; instead of retreating, advance; instead of relaxing, brace anew your nerves for the conflict. Take the whole armor of God. Look upward for grace and strength to wield it. March forward to the "wicket-gate," and to the glory that lies beyond. Keep your eye steadily on the Captain of your salvation. Where his banners wave, be you found, though it be in the thickest of the fight; and soon, yes, soon, your trials will be over; your victory will be won; and you will have naught to do but to lay aside your weapons, and sing the note of eternal triumph.

LETTER VII.

FAITH ESSENTIAL TO PRAYER.

In my last, I recommended earnestness and sincerity, as necessary to acceptable prayer. The third particular which I mentioned was, *faith* in the promises.

Does not your Bible, my young friend, insist upon this? Does it not declare, that he who cometh to God, "must believe that he is, and that he is the rewarder of them that diligently seek him?" Does it not compare to the fluctuation of the restless wave, that prayer which is offered without faith? And does it not assert, that without faith, it is impossible to please him? But what is meant by faith in the promises? methinks I hear you say. How shall I know when I incorporate this faith in my petition? It is not necessary, my young friend, that you know it; but it is necessary, and even indispensable, that you have it.

There is afloat, a spurious and vain-confident feeling, that mistakes presumption for faith. This sometimes appears in communities which are visited by the special influences of the Holy Spirit. Ignorant and proud enthusiasts take advantage of excited feelings, and sow the tares of error, while the servant of Jesus is scattering the seeds of truth. Some have declared, that in praying for a blessing, we had only to believe that it would be granted, and success was certain. In praying for an individual, all we had to do was to be certain in our own minds that the individual would be converted, and it would be so. When I look at the spirit which such people evince, and find little of the meekness and humility of the Gospel, I view it as presumptive evidence against their characters, and their opinions. When David prayed for the life of his child, though with deep humility and earnestness, it was not spared. When Paul thrice besought the Lord for the removal of a grievous affliction, the prayer was heard, and answered on the soul; but not as he had expected, on the body. The prayer of faith is never lost. It is invariably answered. But to assert that it will be answered in the particular way, or for the particular thing which we have expected, is both antiscriptural and presumptuous. Here lies the error of these enthusiasts. One step farther would make them claim inspiration.

When we come to the throne of grace, we come, not to dictate, but to supplicate. God, in his word, has given us a warrant to pray for all spiritual, and many temporal favors. In praying for the former, we may, and must be importunate and persevering until death. In respect to the latter, we must be submissive; and ever add, If it will be for thy glory, and the interests of my soul. When you pray, therefore, for spiritual blessings, you know that your prayer is according to the will of God. If it be sincere, and presented with an exclusive reference to the mediation of Christ, it will, it must be answered. I do not say, that the very things you ask, and in the precise way and time in which you look for them, will be received. Not at all. But still I say, your prayer will be answered. We are short-sighted creatures. We often suppose that we know what is best for us, and would fain have in our own hands the management of our spiritual and temporal affairs. But recollect the "ring." It is not for us to keep it. It is in the hands of God. There only is it safe. There, no foe can reach it, and no fears need be entertained of its security.

Recollect, then, that it is yours to believe. It is God's to plan and to execute. Confidence in God's veracity, and wisdom, and goodness, is the main ingredient in this prayer of faith. Say, in the fulness of your confidence, I plead for this thing, O God. Although it may not be given by thee in a manner, and at a time which I expect, still I plead thy promise; and I know thou art faithful to hear and answer prayer.

Permit me to recur again to my own experience, and I am not alone in this experience. Knowing that I was in a backslidden state, and feeling that for months there had been a melancholy distance between God and my soul, I gave myself to prayer. I entreated God to reclaim me, to give me repentance, and a more entire consecration of soul and body to his service. I knew that these were blessings which were according to the will of God, and I knew that he had promised in his word to answer prayer for such blessings. With the hope that I entertained of being in covenant with him, how could I doubt that he would answer the prayer for sanctification? But I verily supposed, that it would be by a direct influence of the Spirit on the heart. I expected that, in some favored moment, perhaps while I was then praying, God would send down a holy influence, irradiate the darkened mind, melt the hard heart, purify the sordid affections, and arrest and reclaim the wanderer. This he might have done. This he sometimes does in the case of others; but it was not thus he answered my prayer.

When that season of earnest supplication had passed away, and was almost forgotten, he stretched me upon a bed of affliction, and filled my mind with darkness, and my body with torturing pains. Every expedient was tried to alleviate, but the waves and the billows rolled deeper and darker. Why is it, I was then led to inquire, that God's hand is pressed so heavily upon me? Look back, my soul, upon thy pride, thy worldly-mindedness, thy ambition, thy sensuality, thy neglect of duty. Do not these compose the cloud that envelopes thee; are they not the pains that rack thee? Hast thou not forsaken " the Fountain of living waters?" Then, like the prodigal's, my eyes were filled with penitential tears; and I said, God is answering my prayer for humility, for spirituality, for meekness, for more entire devotedness.

Happy is that soul who can say, Oh Lord, sanctify me, if it be by fire. Sanctify me, even if it be through the deep waters of affliction.

I cite this example to show, that our prayers must be offered, and offered in confidence. But the way and the time of their being answered, it is not for us to dictate. We may take any promise in the word of God, and with the confidence of children go to him, and say, Our Father, hast thou not said thus, and dost thou not say this to me? Let me then remind thee, O thou covenant-keeping God, of these ample promises, and let me beseech thee to fulfil them all in thy servant; and in thine own way let them be verified in my complete salvation.

LETTER VIII.

FOR WHAT SHOULD WE PRAY?

It was not my intention to extend my remarks to so great a length on the nature of prayer, but I have been insensibly led along by my anxiety to impress upon your mind the importance of the subject. By personal experience I have, I trust, learned its value. I have been able to trace every spiritual declension to the closet. When the enemies of my soul have triumphed, I could distinctly see that my armor had not been furbished by prayer. When the sweet serenity of conscious forgiveness, a calm sense of divine favor has departed, and the restless tumult of passion has succeeded, the Holy Spirit, I knew full well, had not, with fervency, been wooed to my bosom.

As well might we expect vegetation to spring from the earth without the sunshine or the dew, as the Christian to unfold his graces, and advance in his course, without patient, persevering, and ardent prayer. The throne of grace must be your home, your dearest, happiest home. If unavoidably detained from your accustomed visits to the sweet retreat, O may you feel, like the dove that fluttered anxiously around the ark, that on earth there is naught that is stable, on which to rest your weary foot. And when you again find the consecrated spot, may your tears of joy mingle with those of penitence, as you throw yourself anew into the arms of your Father and your Friend.

In my last, I spoke of praying with faith in the promises, so that I have now glanced at the three important particulars necessary in acceptable prayer

The second inquiry, *for what* you should pray, needs, it appears to me, but little consideration, if you have been taught of the Spirit. The apostle says, " we know not what we should pray for as we ought," but " the Spirit helpeth our infirmities." It would not, therefore, become me to enumerate the particulars which should form the subject matter of your prayers. If the Holy Spirit has wrought in your soul a deep conviction of your depravity, you will wrestle with God for its removal. " Create in me a clean heart, O God, and renew a right spirit within me." If you are suddenly betrayed into sin, and your conscience feel the heavy load, you will exclaim, " O Lord, pardon mine iniquity, for it is great." If your heart be sluggish in duty, you will, of course, and from necessity, pray, " Quicken me, O Lord, and I will run in the ways of thy commandments." If you love the kingdom of Christ, you will pray earnestly, and with faith, for its coming. If you feel for the perishing condition of sinners, you will commend them, with tears, to the mercy of your God.

But your prayers will not be thus general. If you ever, as I trust you will, become a noble and devoted Christian; if you mean to put your feet in the warm tracks of a Newell or a Huntington, your prayers will often be protracted and particular. You will pray for blessings on your own soul, on your parents, on your sisters, on your neighborhood, on the world. Your ardent mind, steeped in benevolence, will hold a familiar and holy intercourse with your Father in heaven. Not an anxiety will you feel, but you will communicate it; not a reasonable wish will you indulge, but you will express it; not a known duty will you discover, but you will pray for grace to perform it. To enter into further particulars would be unnecessary. The Christian has every day new sins to confess, new duties to perform, new temptations to encounter; requiring, of course, new modifications of prayer and praise.

But one subject let me entreat you never to forget. It is the rising glory of our Immanuel's kingdom. Say, with David, or rather with those weeping captives who were mingling their tears with the waters of Babylon, "If I forget thee, O Jerusalem, let my right hand forget her cunning: if I do not remember thee, let my tongue cleave to the roof of my mouth; if I prefer not Jerusalem above my chief joy." You live in a day of wonders. Your being, perhaps, has opened in the millennial morn. It is possible you may live to see its full-orbed splendors. O, then, in every prayer remember Zion; remember the heathen who sit in the valley and shadow of spiritual death. Take an enlarged view of this subject; read the promises which secure to our Redeemer the whole habitable globe; peruse them until your soul is fired with the prospect. Then go to the mercy-seat and plead for their fulfilment. Go, bear on your heart a sinking world. Let your whole soul be drawn forth on this glorious subject. If it be not your lot to carry the glad tidings to the benighted, sustain, by your prayers, the hands and the hearts of those whose are the privilege and the glory. Say not, I am a poor insignificant creature; what will my prayers avail? Ah, if every Christian were thus to reason, the church would be without prayer, and without a blessing. Have you an interest at the throne of grace in your own behalf? Do you hope so; and, believing so, do you act accordingly? then have you also an interest there in behalf of a perishing world. That interest you must use. By all the prospective glories of the Messiah, I beseech you to use it. By all the deep and inconceivable miseries of the heathen, by the probability of their condemnation, and by the possibility of their deliverance, I conjure you to use it. Whatever you forget, forget not the millions who are perishing for lack of vision. Forget not the self-denied missionary who has gone to relieve them;

forget not the societies which are pledged to this holy enterprise. The day is coming when this subject will hold a prominence in our supplications; when the prayer, "Thy kingdom come," will come gushing from the heart, and be reiterated with an earnestness which shall indicate its near approach, and be prophetic of its universality.

You see from my protracted remarks on this subject, that I consider prayer the life and soul of the Christian. To the young Christian I cannot too urgently press its importance. Prayer is the key of heaven. O, what has it not done? By it Elijah shut up the skies, and no dew nor rain descended on the guilty land. By it Jacob placed a ladder between heaven and earth, and formed a communication for angels. By it Daniel shut up the mouths of ferocious lions, Sampson shook the pillars of Philistia's temple, and Peter was delivered from prison. Prayer is a mighty weapon in the hands of the weakest. Use it, then; never, O never yield up this weapon.

In my next I shall offer a few remarks on the third question, when should we pray?

LETTER IX.

WHEN SHOULD WE PRAY?

I shall make but a few additional observations, my young friend, on the subject of prayer, although, I confess, my pen would pursue the delightful theme through many pages more.

The apostle commands us to "pray *without ceasing*." Are we by this to understand that every moment of our time is to be spent in prayer? This, undoubtedly, is not his meaning. The import of the exhortation is, omit not this important duty; be regular and punctual in your daily visits to the altar; and see to it that you continually preserve a prayerful frame of spirit. No person can plead for a more strict interpretation of the passage than this. It implies all that the apostle meant to inculcate; and, be assured, that if you persevere in such a course, you will not subject yourself to the charge of "casting off fear, and restraining prayer before God."

The seasons of prayer are stated and occasional, ordinary and extraordinary. No Christian can maintain a close walk with God, none can keep alive the hallowed fire of the soul, without daily kindling it afresh at the altar. None can grow in knowledge and holiness without stated and regular seasons of prayer "Give us this day our daily bread," implies as much the aliment of the soul as the nourishment of the body. The one can no more live in health and vigor without prayer, than the other without food.

It is usual to recommend the morning and the evening, as the most suitable seasons for prayer. In this, I fully concur. There appears to be something peculiarly appropriate in this arrangement of duty.

When the darkness has passed, and the light has again dawned upon the earth; when we rise from our couch, and find our faculties invigorated by the restoring slumbers of the night; when we view the beauties of the morning landscape, listen to the melody of birds, and feel the balmy breath of nature playing coolly and sweetly around us; when praise and thanksgiving to God seem inscribed upon every feature of a revived world: how can we be silent; how withhold the burst of rapturous adoration? These scenes, I am aware, awaken no such feelings in the hearts of multitudes. They gaze on them, it is true; but they recognize not the hand that formed them. They feel no thrill of gratitude, nor offer one note of praise. Not so with the Christian. To him they convey a lesson, through the eye, to the soul; and lead him "from nature, up to nature's God."

How proper, then, my young friend, is the morning, for secret converse with your God. It is your privilege to reside in the country. You live amid nature's magnificence. The unobstructed arch of heaven is your canopy. For your eye the forest waves, the meadows smile, the garden unfolds its beauties, and spring and summer vie in their efforts to regale your senses. You are not crowded into a noisy and profligate city, and shut out from almost every thing that is pleasant to the eye, and calming to the soul. No; you dwell, as it were, with God, and among his glorious works. Let your first hours, therefore, be his. Let not sloth nail you to your couch, when all nature invites you to awake and join the general concert of praise. "Awake, psaltery and harp," must be your language; "I myself will awake early." Mary found her way to the sepulchre ere the day dawned; nor wept at that sepulchre in vain.

Early devotions are all-important. They prepare the mind to attend, without distraction, to the secular duties of the morning. As the day breaks, summon your recollections, and rise with the rising light. Give your first hours to God. Pour out your soul before him in gratitude for nocturnal blessings, and throw yourself on his protection for the day. Be assured, this early application to his throne will distil upon the soul a peace and a serenity that shall not depart, but shall gild every look and action, and make the day glide onward smoothly and happily.

You will thus allow yourself time, and not be hurried in your prayers. You will also be free from interruptions, and the fear of them. This is all-important to a right discharge of sacred duties. It is indispensable that the mind should be free from solicitude and cares : and there is no time in the day that will so secure to you that freedom, as the early part of it.

Arise so early as to allow yourself half an hour for the performance of your morning devotions : more, if your soul desire it. It is good to stipulate with yourself for half an hour. The devotions of many are insipid, and burdensome, and unacceptable, because they have no definite time allotted for their performance. They snatch a few moments in the morning, and hurry through a form of prayer ; which, though for the time it may pacify the conscience, yet, in the end, only increases their guilt. They do not make a business of prayer. This is the great reason why the exercise is a burden. Now, avoid this, my young friend, by having an early hour, and always occupying the full time, in a constant and conscientious attention to your devotional duties. You will find by experience, that there is a great advantage in being thus systematic. It will tend greatly to elevate your standard of piety, and make you, not a lean and desultory, but a consistent and growing Christian.

In your evening devotions, I should advise you to occupy, as a general rule, as much time as in the morning. I know that circumstances must be regarded; but I would endeavor to secure at least half an hour in the evening. Let this hour not be the last before retiring; because, generally, the body is too much wearied, and the mind, by sympathy, too drowsy to make devotion any thing but a task and a burden. Let it be early in the evening. If the hour of sunset is most convenient, let it be then. This was the time at which the patriarch Isaac was engaged in meditation and prayer, and it certainly is a very appropriate and delightful hour.

How proper and pleasant is it to sit down at evening, and review the mercies of the day, call in the thoughts from distracting occupations, and then pour the whole soul into the bosom of God. How delightful to seek our pillow, when, having bathed anew in the fountain of Immanuel's blood, we feel a consciousness of pardon, and a hope full of immortality. Our slumbers then are sweet and refreshing. No visions of guilt, no fearful anticipations distort the unconscious muscles, or heave the troubled bosom. These are the tortures of guilty impenitence. They are the scourges of a conscience unpacified by the blood of atonement—the forebodings of that dreadful doom that awaits all who continue unreconciled to God, by the death of his Son.

One more letter shall close my remarks on this subject.

LETTER X.

PRAYER—CONCLUDED.

A Christian who aims at an elevated standard of piety, will not always be satisfied with the morning and evening sacrifice.

The most eminent Christians have followed the example of David, who, in asserting his perseverance in prayer, exclaims, " Evening, and morning, and at noon will I pray." And is this too much ? I am persuaded, my young friend, that to a soul who pants after increasing conformity to God, it is not too much. It may not always be convenient to pray three times a day, but where it is, I promise the individual, he will be no loser by the exercise. The aliment of the body may be taken too often, and in too great quantities, for the health of the constitution : but not so that of the soul. There is no danger of satiety or repletion here. You may drink, and drink again, at the waters of life; you may banquet, and return again and banquet. The soul will thrive proportionably. The food, instead of being loathed, will have the keener relish, and administer increasing nourishment, until you grow up to the stature of the perfect in Christ Jesus.

A Christian of exalted piety will carry a prayerful frame of spirit throughout the day. He will not make his stated devotions the beginning and the ending of his religion. Such is the conduct of the hypocrite, and the formalist. But the Christian imbibes a portion of heaven, which he continually carries in his countenance, and exhibits in his deportment. Though walking amid the avocations of secular life, he still walks with God. As a matter of duty, he descends from his elevation to perform his part in the concerns of this sublunary world; but his soul is not here. His higher affections are calmly ascending to God. The silent ejaculation supplies his necessary absence from the throne of grace; and is, if you will allow me the comparison, a sort of informal repast to the soul.

The most eminent saints have been noted for frequent ejaculatory petitions. A temptation suddenly shoots across the mind—send upward the silent prayer for deliverance. You are about entering into dangerous circumstances—look upward for protection. Your feet have just touched the threshold of God's temple—O then breathe upward for his Spirit and his presence. If your soul be attuned to devotion, you will live and breathe as in the presence of God, and travel through this wilderness leaning on the arm of your beloved.

In addition to this, I would urge the duty of extraordinary and special seasons of prayer. I find such seasons warranted by the Scriptures, and their importance attested by the experience of the most eminent saints, in all ages of the church. There are lapses of the soul, which can only be counteracted by special and extraordinary prayer. There are temptations, which at times so beset and harass the mind as to call for special means. There are afflictive dispensations which require them. There are perplexities as to the path of duty, which they only can remove. Hence, if you will note the biography of the most eminently pious, you will find that special seasons of fasting, humiliation, and prayer, have been accompanied with an increase of grace, a deeper acquaintance with the heart, a more spiritual intercourse with God, more glorious views of divine truth, and a surer hope of a blessed immortality.

I think I can say, without hesitation, that the most exalted attainments have been made by such means Such extraordinary seasons of prayer are peculiarly acceptable to God. It was such, accompanied by a sanctifying influence, that formed the high character of Brainerd, and of Martyn.

If you desire their piety, neglect not the means by which they attained to it. If you admire their character, then imitate their devotion and self-denial. There is no obstacle that may not be surmounted, to hinder you even from outstripping them. The prize is before you. The race is pointed out. See, at its termination, a crown of glory beaming in your Saviour's hands. Does it not fire your soul? Does it not fill your eye? Does it not brace anew your nerves? Fix your eye on the mark of the prize of your high calling. Consider all the ground you have passed as nothing, so long as the goal is still at a distance—so long as you come short of perfection in Christ Jesus.

But I have one remark before I dismiss this subject. It is this. Let nothing, if possible, hinder you, in the performance of your regular devotions, from occupying your allotted season of prayer. When the love of God is on the wane, and that of the world is waxing stronger, a trifling excuse will satisfy the conscience for the neglect of this all-important duty. May such never be your case. Such a state is replete with danger, and often a precursor to a melancholy and disgraceful fall. The soul that is bent on duty, and to whom prayer is a delightful privilege, will seldom be hindered from its performance. No trifling excuse will be heeded; and if necessity for a time bar up the sacred enclosure, the heart will sicken at the void which is created by a temporary absence from the hallowed spot. When that necessity can be removed, how will the soul leap forward to its dearest earthly home. It will seem doubly sweet for the temporary hinderance. The soul will say, as it lays itself beneath the altar, O blessed privilege; how long does it appear since I last enjoyed thee. How delightful to lay my head on this dear support, and feel that I am again alone with my Redeemer and my friend.

Such will be the language of the saint when debarred for a time from the throne of grace.

Situated as you now are, you are in a measure free from the fear of such interruptions. But you will soon be ushered into a new sphere. You will soon find yourself surrounded by companions, to whom you must pay the ordinary civilities of life. Then will you need this advice; nay, you will need the supporting hand of God, to keep you from dishonoring your profession, and forgetting the solemn vows you have recorded. Then, if you persevere in the course which I have marked out, it will be evident that I have not written in vain, and that what I have written has been attended with more than human efficacy.

Little do you know, as yet, of your own heart; little do you realize the seducing influence of the world, and the artful insinuations of Satan. But if you will cling to the counsel I have given, and commit your soul to the keeping of your Redeemer, those temptations you shall meet immovable as the rock that beats back the angry billow—you shall walk unhurt amid the flames—you shall be covered with a panoply impervious to attack—you shall weather out the storm in safety—and at last, when your temptations and trials are over, you shall sing, eternally sing "Unto Him who hath loved me, and washed me from my sins in his own blood; to him be glory and dominion for ever and ever."

LETTER XI.

SELF-EXAMINATION.

You will recollect, my young friend, that I proposed to direct you to the attainment of an elevated standard of piety. In the course of my remarks, you must ever bear in mind that I am suggesting only the important means and methods of such attainment. Ever recollect, that without the Spirit's influence, the Christian can no more advance in holiness, than the sinner repent and believe; and yet the former will be guilty for not advancing, and the latter for not complying with the demands of the Gospel.

The three grand helps towards the point at which you aim, are prayer, self-examination, and a close and diligent perusal of the Scriptures. The first topic has been already discussed. Imperfectly as it has been set forth, I trust you are deeply convinced of its importance; and I shall, therefore, briefly attend to the second, namely, SELF-EXAMINATION.

This is a duty as difficult as it is important. Every Christian acknowledges it to be so. The object of self-examination is to obtain a correct knowledge of our moral character. Before conversion, man is generally a stranger to himself. As he comes forth from the nursery, he enters upon the reckless career of boyhood. His eye and ear are all attention, as one object after another crowds upon his view. He is full of interrogatories concerning the phenomena both of art and of nature. He courts every trifle; and when obtained, throws it away in pursuit of another. But he watches not the operations of his own mind. He is, indeed, all attention to the busy world without; but all inattention to the busy world within. And such will he continue to be when boyhood shall give place to maturity, unless the Holy Spirit turn his eye inward on the soul. A philosopher, he may range through nature, and collect and classify her productions, and yet never sit one solitary hour in severe judgment on himself. Such a man is, in one sense, a wise man, but in another a fool. That he is a man of knowledge, no one acquainted with his attainments can deny; but, in my opinion, he is far from being a man of wisdom, in the highest and noblest use of that term.

> "Knowledge and wisdom, far from being one,
> Have ofttimes no connection. Knowledge dwells
> In heads replete with thoughts of other men;
> Wisdom in minds attentive to their own.
> Knowledge is proud that he has learned so much;
> Wisdom is humble that he knows no more."

It is surprising how few persons are in the habit of attending to the operations of their own minds The generality of mankind are so absorbed in the various pursuits of life, that no opportunity is allowed for serious introspection. They live in a whirlpool of cares; and to them, the deeper and more boisterous the vortex, the better. They are all hurry and bustle; business and pleasure swallow up every thought; and thus life's important hours, like successive couriers, chase each other into eternity. Hence, you will often find these gay dreamers, when brought to a death-bed, taking, for the first time, a direct and dreadful look at themselves. Life has been frittered away, and eternity now stares them into a consciousness of their ruin.

The Christian who is taught of the Spirit, is the only man who can be said to be acquainted with himself. Not that he can notice every hue of moral feeling; nor can he comprehend the "mystery of iniquity" that pervades the heart: for it is "deceitful above all things; who can know it?" But he is so much in the habit of noticing his moral exercises; he so frequently communes with his own heart, that he comes at length to an acquaintance with himself, and can pronounce, with humble confidence, on his present state and his future destiny. Such a character is venerable and immovable. Changes may occur; prosperity or adversity may come; but he walks in too high a region to be unduly elated by the former, or sinfully depressed by the latter. What a calm, delightful, enviable summit. It is like the mountain covered with verdure, upon whose top rest the mild beams of glory; whilst, in the figurative language of Goldsmith, the "midway storm" thunders and rages beneath.

We are expressly enjoined by the apostle to "examine ourselves"—to "know our own selves;" for by so doing we come to the knowledge of our true characters. If we are Christians, we may, and we must endeavor to know it. Such knowledge will remove our fears, and add greatly to our comfort. Some, I am well aware, walk in darkness and in doubt to the end of their journey. They see no light until heaven's glory breaks in upon the soul. Such, no doubt, was the case of the amiable and pious Cowper; but his case was a peculiar one.

In general, the knowledge of his personal salvation is attainable by the Christian. None should ever think of resting until such assurance is attained. It may not be the will of God to give it, but it is his will that we should strive for it. If you aim at an elevated standard of piety, this will be your mark.

Some persons are satisfied with just enough of religion to ease the conscience and give encouragement for a feeble hope. They never rise above this grade, nor ever manifest more than a sort of negative character. Self-examination they utterly neglect; or, if they pretend to practise it, they perform the duty so seldom and superficially, as to depress, rather than elevate, their own low and diminutive standard.

Be thou not of their number. Employ every means to become thoroughly acquainted with your true character. Make religion your grand business. Let the soul be the all-absorbing subject of interest. How dreadful would it be to pass into eternity with false hopes and mistaken views. Determine to know the worst as well as the best of your case. Come to a personal investigation with the spirit of an inflexible inquisitor. Go into the secret chambers of the soul, and carry thither the touchstone of salvation, the torch of truth.

In my next I hope to enter a little more minutely into this subject. In the mean time I commend you to the grace of Him who is able to build you up—to enable you to go from strength to strength—to fire your flagging zeal—rouse the animating hope—and put within you the spirit of a self-denying a devoted Christian.

LETTER XII.

SELF-EXAMINATION, STATED AND OCCASIONAL.

The duty of self-examination, like that of prayer, is both stated and occasional. The conscientious Christian should not suffer a single day to pass, without an investigation of his moral character. At the close of the day, and when about to commit the keeping of his soul to Him "who never slumbereth nor sleepeth," he should take a deliberate and serious retrospect of the past. His conduct, and the motives which prompted it, should pass under investigation.

I cannot, my young friend, too strongly recommend to you this practice. The most eminent saints have been distinguished for it, and I must press upon you a similar course, if you would aim at an elevated standard of piety.

There is less difficulty attending this diurnal investigation, than many professors imagine. Were long intervals to occur between the periods of self-examination, we should indeed experience much inconvenience and perplexity in performing the duty. We should then resemble the unskilful and heedless merchant, who, yielding to habitual negligence and hurry, defers posting his books until he is overwhelmed with their intricacy and magnitude. But let the duty be daily and thoroughly performed, and we rise to the standard of the skilful and prudent merchant, who duly records every item of business; who never closes his counting-house, until his balance-sheet is made up; and who, by a single reference, can tell the true state of his accounts, and form a correct estimate of his commercial standing.

You will find yourself aided in this work by a secret journal or diary, which must be excluded from the inspection of all but God and yourself.

If you are in the habit of thus daily inquiring into your motives and conduct, you will find it an excellent preparation for approaching a throne of grace. You will perceive so many failures in duty, and such frequent commission of sin, that your soul must necessarily be humbled before God. You will also perceive whether you make any advances in knowledge and holiness, and thus discover a source of encouragement, or a stimulus to greater diligence. Your conscience will be rendered tender and faithful; and you will thus be on the alert, that you be not tempted, or drawn aside from your duty. You will walk softly amid the thorny path, nor feel the bleeding wounds which are inflicted on so many careless and worldly-minded professors.

Besides this daily process which I am recommending, there is one special season of self-examination which you should by no means omit. The apostle enjoins on every Christian, to examine himself before he partakes of the Lord's supper. "Let a man examine himself, and so let him eat of that bread, and drink of that cup." This is indispensable to a profitable attendance on this interesting and significant ordinance. If you are in the habit of daily self-examination, you will find the observance of this special season by no means difficult or laborious. You will have acquired, by your daily introspection, so much self-knowledge—such a tact, if I may be allowed the expression, at seizing upon evidence, and analyzing feelings and motives, that instead of proving an unwelcome task, it will constitute a satisfactory, comforting, and delightful duty.

The reason why so many complain of the difficulty of a proper discharge of this duty, is obvious. I shall, in a subsequent letter, disclose it more fully.

Be assured, my young friend, that if ever you arrive at an elevated standard of piety, you will attribute it as much to a strict and persevering self-examination, as to any other means which it is, under God, your privilege to use. It is through a neglect of this, that Christianity makes, in most of us, such a dwarfish appearance. It is for the want of this, that hypocrisy vaunts itself in the habiliments of piety. It is for the want of this, that doubts, and fears, and disquietude, and backslidings, are so prevalent. I entreat you, therefore, as you value your peace and your improvement, to persevere in the faithful discharge of this duty. You will be abundantly rewarded. Faith will walk arm in arm with the promises; hope, instead of a flickering light, will become a steady radiation from an unclouded sun; love will grow to a flame that "many waters cannot quench;" and zeal, founded in truth, and directed by knowledge, will hold on, until death, its vigorous and untiring career.

I say not that you will at once arrive at this lofty elevation. Ah, no; you may have many a thorny path to tread, many a rugged way to traverse, many a difficult hill to climb. Nights of weeping, and days of darkness and of tempest may intervene. But God will interpose in your behalf; he will "temper the wind to the shorn lamb."

Recollect, for your encouragement, that the farther you proceed, the easier and the more delightful will be the passage. As it approximates heaven, it partakes of celestial beauty. Like the fine, free avenue to a noble metropolis, the proximity of this road to the heavenly Jerusalem opens wider, and shows clearer, and almost admits the eager eye to catch the spires of glory as they glitter in the light of heaven. Take up your cross, dear youth, and march forward. While you may encounter difficulties, you may also partake of many pleasures—pleasures which are as much superior to the sickly joys of earth, as the river of life is purer than the green waters of an offensive and stagnant pool.

> "The hill of Zion yields
> A thousand sacred sweets,
> Before we reach the heavenly fields,
> Or walk the golden streets."

To me it has ever appeared strange, that when so much depends on the duty of self-examination, it should be so generally neglected.

We do not thus act in our temporal affairs. If the claim to an estate be attended with any degree of doubt or embarrassment, we spare no pains to give it a thorough investigation. If the body be disordered, we are alive to every symptom, and we watch every new aspect of the disease. But in respect to the soul, we are at little pains to substantiate its hope by actual examination. We live along as if the matter were settled—as if we had a guarantee for our heavenly inheritance; when, in fact, all is doubt and embarrassment—when perhaps we may have only "a name to live, whilst we are dead."

Let this duty, my young friend, be viewed by you as altogether indispensable. Set about it with diligence. Should your enemy, knowing its usefulness and importance, attempt to discourage you, listen not to the voice of the tempter. Renew your labor; call upon God to fix your thoughts, and to give you success. Persevere, even unto death, in a duty so necessary to your safety, and essential to your comfort.

LETTER XIII.

SUPERFICIAL SELF-EXAMINATION.

It was intimated in my last, that I should pursue my remarks a little farther upon self-examination. My reasons for so doing are, the importance of the subject, and the general neglect of it with which many Christians are chargeable.

Since the duty is so intimately connected with your hope of salvation, your advancement in holiness, and your general elevation of character, you will bear with me a little longer, even though the subject should appear to be destitute of those incidental attractions which are peculiar to the ordinary accomplishments of life. You must first lay the solid column; the Corinthian capital may then be superadded. My conscience would condemn me, were I to speak first of external conduct, when the piety of the soul is paramount, and demands the first and deepest consideration. Let this be obtained, and, I doubt not, your manners and deportment will take that elevated and noble character which will secure to you the love of the virtuous, and the respect and admiration of all

Fixing the attention on manners and deportment before the heart is rectified, is like profusely adorning the exterior of a building when it is all unfinished and comfortless within. You are allured by the imposing aspect which it presents; but upon entering, how great is your disappointment to find, not only no correspondence in the interior, but every thing cheerless and forbidding. It is certainly more pleasing, to view even a homely exterior, an outside that promises but little, and to perceive within, beauty, symmetry, and elegance. Happy will you be, if, gifted as you are with at least an agreeable person, you can so irradiate your mind with knowledge and holiness as to throw around you an additional attraction, and make your soul approximate to the comeliness of an unfallen spirit. But I have digressed, and must return.

The difficulty of arriving at a knowledge of our true character, does not arise from any deficiency or obscurity in evidence, as recorded in the word of God, but from the manner of applying that evidence to ourselves. The liability to deception lies here. We cannot say that we have the evidence, because we may have spurious and hypocritical feelings, which our self-love may mistake for genuine Christian emotions. The word of God is full, clear, and explicit. It marks out the true disciple of Christ with unerring exactness. The evidence is direct and indirect, positive and negative, in example or embodied principle.

The direct evidence, is that which consists in a

record of the feelings which every Christian must possess. The Bible is full of this. The indirect, is that which may be inferred from precepts and principles. The positive, is exhibited in all those commands which relate to doing the will of God. The negative, from example or embodied principle, is that which is derived from the conduct of the patriarchal and primitive saints.

Thus, you see the Bible is full of evidence relating to the character of the genuine follower of Christ. That evidence is clear and explicit, presented under various forms, and couched in the simplest phraseology. Where, then, lies the difficulty of correctly ascertaining, at once, our true character? I will tell you. It lies in the depravity of the human heart. That heart, as I have already observed, is "deceitful above all things:" and this is the true reason why we cannot appropriate this evidence, with the certainty of its application.

But I will enter into a few particulars, for your farther satisfaction, to show you that self-examination is as difficult as it is important; and that nothing but a long course of painful, persevering effort, will bring you to a confidence, unshaken by doubt, of your being a child of God, and a joint heir with Jesus Christ. You do not wish to have a name to live, and still be dead. You do not desire to go into eternity with a profession only. No; you wish not

SELF-EXAMINATION.

to be deceived in so momentous an affair; for the world, you would not be deceived. You have counted the cost; you have surveyed the cross; and you are determined to follow your Lord. You will not then be discouraged, when I inform you, that to deal with your own heart, in close examination, is a great and difficult work. But the difficulty, as I before observed, will diminish with diligence.

One great reason why so little satisfaction is obtained in the work, is, that our investigation is not complete. We do not come to it with a determination to be thorough in its performance. Although we acknowledge that there is no duty so difficult, nor any more important; yet there is none, perhaps, more superficially performed. Although our hopes, our peace of mind, our growth in grace, are intimately connected with close self-examination; yet, how easily are we discouraged by obstacles which the enemies of our souls may interpose; and how hastily do we run through the duty, deriving no satisfaction, but only enveloping the mind in still deeper gloom. After one or two such superficial trials, some will give up the duty as impracticable, and live along in doubt, and die, perhaps, in distressing uncertainty.

We are less thorough in this spiritual investigation than we should be in almost any other subject. No wonder, then, that we make such slow advances in self-knowledge; no wonder, that it is generally viewed as impracticable, when so superficially performed. When you, my young friend, enter upon this duty, make, I entreat you, sure work with your soul; explore the secret motives, and analyze the evanescent feelings. If it cost years of persevering labor, ascertain, if possible, whether you have an inheritance on high. May God, by his Spirit, assist you, and make you successful.

LETTER XIV.

SUPERFICIAL SELF-EXAMINATION.

I observed, in my last, that we were in danger of being superficial in the work of self-examination. There will be a strong temptation to this, from our natural indolence, as well as the difficulties to be overcome. Hence, you will find few Christians who make this duty a serious and indispensable business. A little hasty catechizing, just before they celebrate the Lord's supper, is all that is deemed necessary. Two or three months may intervene, during which the soul and its momentous affairs are comparatively neglected. When again summoned to renew their vows over the melting memorials of a Saviour's love, they begin to think of some preparation; but one moment steals upon the heels of another, and the business is deferred until the hour when the inviting bell is calling them to the feast. Then, all is agitation and hurry, when all should be calm, collected, and contemplative. They leave to themselves, perhaps, a few moments, to extricate the soul from a tumult of cares; and after an ineffectual and superficial attempt at self-examination, they go tremblingly in doubt, or fearlessly in cold-hearted presumption.

Such is the character of many who profess to be

aiming at the crown of glory. They do not sit in judgment on the internal man, as did David, when he threw open the chambers of his secret soul, and exclaimed, "Search me, O God, and know my heart; try me, and know my thoughts; and see if there be any wicked way in me, and lead me in the way everlasting." It is mere half-way work with them. Conscience prejudges and condemns. To silence her clamors, it is necessary that they make at least a show of self-examination. But when they take up the sacred record, they find so little there which can be honestly appropriated in their favor, that they are obliged, if they would glean any thing for their encouragement, to misinterpret and misapply its meaning. When they meet with such a sweeping declaration as this, "If any man love the world, and the things that are in the world, the love of the Father is not in him;" when their eyes glance at so discriminating a text, they employ a ready sophistry, to modify its severity, or avert its application.

There is, recollect, a strong temptation to be partial in this important work. Self-love prompts us to look more eagerly for the favorable, than the unfavorable evidence; and gives us a greater readiness in applying the former than the latter. It is an object with our spiritual enemies, to flatter us into a belief of our good estate, that we may omit our watch, and indulge our vain-confident expectations. Thousands are, by this means, led blindfolded down to ruin.

The superficial Christian seizes the most equivocal evidence. It will not take much to persuade him that all is safe. If a vast amount of Scripture is against him, and he can yet find but here and there a single text, whose aspect in his case is, to say the least, doubtful, how eagerly will he grasp it, and cast it into the favorable scale. It is, with him, a principle, to be satisfied with the least possible testimony. He will make one text, which he supposes to be in his favor, neutralize a hundred others which are most unequivocally against him. Hence, you will sometimes hear professing Christians declare, that were it not for this one text, " We know that we have passed from death unto life, because we love the brethren," they should be driven to despair.

This may, indeed, be the language of a sincere disciple; of one who walks in darkness, but who goes mourning over his personal deficiency. Far be it from me to discourage such. This precious text was recorded by the compassionate Spirit for him; and often, when the billows were high, and the prospect all darkness, it has beamed like a star of hope upon his trembling soul, and saved it from despair and death. But when I hear it quoted by a thoughtless, worldly-minded professor, I account it a sad mark against him. Is this the only text to which he can cling? Let him recollect, that the same apostle also said, "By this we know that we love the children of God, when we love God, and keep his commandments."

The superficial professor seems determined, if possible, to make the Bible speak in his favor. He comes not to that infallible touchstone with a sincere desire to probe his heart, to examine the reason of his hope, and to scrutinize the foundation of his confidence. He comes not with a resolution to make thorough and impartial work, but to make the word of God, like the fabled oracles of heathenism, speak a language ambiguous and equivocal.

Now, my young friend, be thou of a different spirit. Go into this investigation with a resolution that you will be thorough and impartial. Say to your Bible, I will consult thee faithfully, thou infallible book. I will let thy light into the darkest chambers of my heart. The sword of the Spirit shall search the system, and probe my wounded nature in the tenderest part. I will not shrink from the inquisition, but will enter upon it sincerely, and persevere in it through life.

LETTER XV.

DANGER OF DECEIVING OURSELVES.

The character of the superficial professor I must carry along with me, in order to show you the importance and the happiness of aiming at a high standard of attainment.

He is a miserable self-deceiver who imagines that any advantage is gained by persuading himself, contrary to evidence, that he is a Christian. And yet there are thousands of this character. Why do they not reflect on God's omniscience? Why do they not consider, that their own good opinion of themselves will not alter their true character. God looketh upon the heart. He strips the outward man, and carries his judicial sentence home upon the soul. He can tear from the heart its most artful disguises, and look with an eye of infallible decision on its emotions. With his "fan in his hand," he will pass through the visible church, "and gather his wheat into the garner; but he will burn up the chaff with unquenchable fire."

He who attends to self-examination superficially, places too much confidence in the judgment of others. Every person knows, that if another's opinion be coincident with our own, we are flattered by it. This is especially the case when it respects our religious character. Some, who are fearful of deception, will, I am well aware, never admit the opinion of others to have any weight. This is certainly the safest extreme. Such are generally mourning Christians, who are much more prone to form an unfavorable, than a flattering opinion of their condition. But others are disposed to place undue reliance on the judgment of those who have expressed the belief that they are Christians. This satisfies them; especially if it be the judgment of those whom they greatly respect, and whose perspicacity as to moral character, they have been in the habit of considering as wellnigh infallible. Perhaps it is merely the wish of a beloved friend, or the expression of parental hope, rather than a deliberate and formal decision upon ascertained evidence; still, it is often enough to undermine the duty of close self-examination, and induce a carelessness, and a confidence, awfully prophetic of deep delinquency, and melancholy backsliding.

It will be evident to you, my young friend, that confidence, if it have no better foundation, is nothing else than presumption; and that it may, ere long, lead to great doubt and perplexity, if not to absolute despair.

The hope of eternal life is not to be taken up on slight grounds. It is a subject to be settled between God and your own soul. I would not despise the advice, nor reject entirely the opinion of others; but I would be careful not to trust too much to such advice and opinion. Since you are to stand or fall by the word of God, it is to that, and to that alone, you must look for testimony in your case. The advice and the opinion of ministers, and private Christians, you will seek and respect; but you will not regard them as infallible, nor place your reliance upon them. Let them neither sink you to despair, nor elevate you to a vain confidence.

You know full well, that no finite being can pronounce with certainty on your spiritual condition. Even the holy apostles, who were under the immediate inspiration of God, were not endued with this prerogative. Were they not deceived respecting the characters of Simon the sorcerer, of Demas, and of others? How, then, can we trust our souls to the opinion of fallible man? What reliance can we place on any thing short of God, and his unerring oracles?

I dwell the longer on this topic, because I have not seen the point brought out fully in any of the experimental treatises which have fallen under my observation; and because there is, in most persons, a strong tendency to lean upon the judgment of others, rather than to be at the pains of a severe and strict investigation for themselves. You cannot be ignorant that such a course must be unsafe and unsatisfactory. How much better to go at once to the Bible. If we there find our character to be that of the saints who have gone before us, what joy and assurance will it give. We know that we are standing on a rock—we feel that it is stable as eternity. But if we lean to human opinion, we shall ever find our evidences equivocal, and our hope neither sure nor steadfast.

Remember, too, my young friend, that those who love us, and who wish us to become Christians, are very liable to be satisfied with the shadow of evidence. They grasp at the first hopeful appearances, and pronounce often a favorable decision when there are not sufficient grounds to warrant it. When you recollect this, you will receive their opinion with the greater hesitancy, and feel more deeply the importance of settling the question over your Bible; between God and your own soul. Man can look only at the outside; his limited vision cannot penetrate within. But God looketh on the heart—on that wandering, wayward heart, the seat of so many joys and sorrows, the abode of so much deceitfulness and impurity. He knows its character. He analyzes its emotions.

To him, therefore, carry your soul, and with David invoke his scrutiny. Then will you be able to give to him that asketh you, "a reason of the hope that is in you, with meekness and fear." Then

SELF-EXAMINATION. 101

you shall have "the peace of God which passeth all understanding." Your title to a heavenly inheritance shall bear the royal signet—a seal which none on earth dare question; and which, when the gates of death shall be unbarred, shall give you free access to the royal presence, and to the temple of God on high. Rest satisfied with nothing short of this seal—and may the Lord enable you to persevere in seeking it.

LETTER XVI.

PAST EXPERIENCES

In prosecuting the work of self-examination, there is another danger to which you will be liable, and against which I would guard you—a reliance upon *past experience*. If you suffer this to have a practical influence upon you, it will palsy every effort, and make you to sit down in indolence, satisfied with present attainments, when you should be pressing towards the mark, for the prize of your high calling.

I mention this, because it is a very common fault, and one but little regarded. What can be pleaded in extenuation of such spiritual sluggishness, I cannot conceive.

The holy apostle who, next to his Lord, is the brightest example which is set before us, counted all his past attainments as nothing, so long as any interval remained between him and the perfection which is in Christ Jesus. Hence, he compares himself to one struggling in a race, reaching forth, and pressing towards the prize which was set before him. What a beautiful figure—reaching forth, pressing towards—mark the expressions.

If you had ever seen an Olympic race, where there were numerous competitors; if you had ever witnoticed their earnestness, as they approached the goal—every muscle strained to the utmost, and the hand reaching forward to seize the crown—you would have a more impressive idea of this beautiful metaphor. May you, by happy experience, know its import. But, my young friend, I fear that there are few, very few of these Olympic strugglers in the Christian race. Too many are satisfied to look on as spectators, while a few only, run and win the prize. Too many loiter in the course, or turn off into the by-paths of iniquity. They base their confidence on past experience. They seem to have settled the point once for all. They will perhaps admit that, as to present evidence of Christian character, they have not much to offer; but they refer you to the time when their evidence was clear and unequivocal. "There was a period," say they, "when we experienced conversion. A great change took place in our feelings, affections, and conduct. We can no more doubt that it was the work of God, than that our bodies are a part of his creation. Others saw and acknowledged the change. 'Tis true, we do not feel now as we did then; but we were told that this abatement of feeling was to be expected—that the ardor of the youthful convert could not last forever." Ask such vain-confident persons for the evidence of their faith, and they refer you immediately to this antedated hope. They are at no pains to inquire for the present evidences of their being in a state of salvation. The business was settled years ago. Others, who will not go quite to this length, will secretly feed their hopes too much upon the past, instead of inquiring into present marks of grace. It is a sad proof that they are either deceived with false appearances, or declining from God and from duty.

I do not mean by these remarks to imply that we are never to recur to past experience for hope and consolation. I believe we are permitted, by the word of God, and the examples of his saints, so to do. David, in a time of deep trouble, said, "I will remember thee, from the land of Jordan, from the Hermonites, and from the hill Mizar."

But what I wish to guard you against, my young friend, is placing too much confidence in the past, and suffering it to operate as an opiate to present vigilance and activity. Past experience is one of the devil's lures to vain confidence; one of the veriest subterfuges of hypocrisy; one of the most common and fatal grounds of self-deception. Even Paul would not trust to the past, although he had been struck blind by a beatific vision of his Master, and introduced into his kingdom under circumstances so striking and peculiar. No; forgetting all that is past, "he presses towards the mark for the prize of his high calling in Christ Jesus."

These old hopes, this former experience, you can

not depend upon. As well might you think of crossing the ocean in a worm-eaten vessel. While the weather was mild, and the sea calm, you might float in apparent security; but should the heavens grow dark, and the billows begin to beat upon the vessel, you would fall a speedy prey to the all-devouring wave. The Christian who has no better basis than by-gone experience to rest upon, may live on, amid the sunshine of life, in apparent ease and comfort; but in that hour when God taketh away the soul, he will long for something more substantial to cling to than a doubtful and antedated hope.

Many are thus fatally deceived. To them life seems to glide onward undisturbed, and the soul is rocked asleep on the pillow of past experience. Conscience may be so far stupefied as not even to arouse at the call of death. They may knock at heaven's gate, but they may also hear the dread voice within, "I know you not; depart from me, ye workers of iniquity."

Such self-deceivers will not acknowledge the duty of daily self-examination. It is impossible to rouse them to the performance of it. They are cased in an impervious mail. They have, in this past experience, an antidote to every fear, and an apology for every delinquency. O, be thou not of their number. Look for daily evidence of salvation. It is present evidences that are called for, and such cannot be given without a daily, habitual self-examination. In all your past experience, there is, to say the least, a possibility of your having been deceived; it is therefore not a sufficient ground of trust. You must be ready now, "to give to him that asketh, the reason of the hope that is within you." If you pursue the course which I have marked out, you shall never need to bring forward an old and antedated hope as the only evidence of your faith, but in every look, and word, and action, you shall make it certain to all, that you are, in deed and in truth, a Christian.

LETTER XVII.

SUPERFICIAL SELF-EXAMINATION.

Assurance of salvation, or even a well-grounded, uniform, and scriptural hope, is a blessing which is not attained by a superficial and infrequent self-examination. It is not generally enjoyed until after a series of persevering and well-applied exertions. Sometimes, where there *is* a desire to be thorough and diligent, it is not enjoyed. It appears to be the will of God, that some should go weeping after it, even to the grave. But generally, if Christians are faithful, they will arrive at a confirmed and satisfactory hope of eternal life.

There is difficulty, I admit, in the work of self-examination. "Even the righteous are scarcely saved—saved, in many instances, as by fire." The heart is so deceitful, and the enemies of our soul so full of evil machinations, that we are liable to draw too favorable conclusions of our being in a state of salvation. There are times, too, when we seem afraid to uncover our bosoms to the piercing glance of God. Like merchants who are on the borders of insolvency, we shrink from making a thorough investigation of our accounts. We tremble at the thought of finding ourselves spiritual bankrupts, and are almost willing, if I may be allowed the comparison, to forge evidences in our favor, and to our own deception.

This is especially the character of one who is not habitually and daily engaged in the work of self-examination. There is an uncertainty and confusion about his hopes, which make him afraid to enter too deeply into the state of his circumstances. He does not open the Bible, and appeal to its searching truths. He fears that the scrutiny would sweep down his cherished expectations. He is, therefore, tempted to hunt out only those portions of Scripture which appear to favor his case, and to blind his vision to those which would shake his confidence, or eradicate his hopes. When he would examine himself respecting the love or the renunciation of sin, he is far from being a thorough and impartial censor. He can yield up some of the least-loved sinful habits, and can give full credit to himself for the self-denial; but the "right hand" and the "right eye" are not parted with. Some worldly project is in view, which militates against too severe a standard of religious character, and which would be found to be inconsistent by too close an application to Bible ethics. Accordingly, instead of making the world yield to the claims of Christianity, he must narrow down Christianity to accommodate the world.

Business, pleasure, and love of reputation, when

they get the ascendency, make self-examination an irksome and unpleasant duty. When a Christian professor is too eager in pursuit of them, he always feels a conviction of delinquency, depriving him of that free and noble air which is ever the concomitant of an approving conscience, and filling his mind with feeble apologies for himself, or with unjust censures against his superiors in piety.

Now, can such a person come fearlessly up to the work of self-examination? Can he take the Bible in his hand, and appeal to the heart-searching God? Can he be a faithful inquisitor of the internal man? Will he not gloss over his sin? Will he not hunt for evidence to neutralize his guilt?

Such a character is satisfied with just enough of religion to make him respectable here, and afford a vague hope of happiness hereafter. But, alas, he is disappointed in both. He is viewed as hypocritical and insincere by many of his fellow-men; and there is great reason to apprehend, that when God cometh to "make up his jewels," he will be found, not among them, but with unbelievers, in the regions of despair.

It is by exhibiting to your view, my young friend, this superficial and flimsy Christianity, that I would warn you against it, and rouse you to diligence in aiming at an elevated standard of piety. Whilst there are difficulties connected with the performance of Christian duties, difficulties of no common magnitude, they are still not insurmountable. The timid and the hesitating shrink and despond; but the true child of God knows that he has enlisted in a warfare that cannot end but with life. When he puts his hand to God's covenant, when he gives his name to the Captain of his salvation, it is a deliberate and well-considered act. He has counted the cost. He has surveyed the enemy; and whilst he acknowledges his own feebleness, he confides in that pledged assistance and protection which will render him invincible and triumphant.

I hope that you have thus considered the subject, and determined to make a thorough and well-disciplined disciple. I trust, that with you, religion shall be all in all. It must be the business of every day; it must be the business of life.

It is a grand mistake to suppose that the superficial Christian can possess spiritual enjoyments. They are not for him. They are for the laborious, the self-denied, the pains-taking Christian. It is the soldier who sleeps in his armor, springs to his post at a word, rushes into the thickest of the fight, and deals his well-directed blows upon the enemy—it is he, and he alone, upon whom his admiring commander bestows the meed of honor, and the trophies of victory.

Be it yours to imitate him in the spiritual conflict, and it shall be yours to share, like him, in the rewards

SELF-EXAMINATION. 111

of conquest: and even far before him shall you be honored, for you shall sit at the King's table, and partake of the rich provisions of his temple. Every thing urges you to diligence and to duty; your honor and your happiness, your safety and your reward. O then, forgetting the things which are behind, reach forth, press onward, and the prize, the glorious prize, shall be soon and for ever yours.

LETTER XVIII.

SELF-EXAMINATION—CONTINUED.

SELF-EXAMINATION respects both *feeling* and *conduct*. A difficulty occurs in ascertaining whether the former is according to the spirit, and the latter correspondent with the precepts of the Bible. I am persuaded that you are already impressed with the importance of the duty, and are resolved that it shall occupy a prominent place in the daily exercises of the closet.

But methinks I hear you inquire in what way you are to proceed; how you are to know that you pursue the duty to advantage; and whether you are not, after all, liable to deception. I have already forewarned you of difficulties which will appear formidable, and which, at the very threshold of your Christian course, will be thrown in your way, to arrest your progress, and frighten you from the discharge of duty. But be not discouraged nor intimidated. Repeated efforts in prayer to God, will enable you to breast the opposition; and that which at first appeared fraught with difficulties, will be found, after a few incipient discouragements, easy and delightful.

Satan will exert his utmost power to hinder you

from this all-important duty. He knows how much your hopes, and your advancement in holiness, depend upon the faithful discharge of it. Having in so many other cases succeeded in hindering its performance, he will hope in yours to succeed. May the grace of God enable you to disappoint him. May you persevere, even amid discouragements, until the duty shall become to you a most precious privilege.

When you enter upon this work, you will first look upward to heaven, in a few short petitions, that God would grant you his Holy Spirit; that he would fix your attention on the immediate duty before you; that he would keep you from a superficial investigation, and enable you to deal closely and thoroughly with your heart.

We are very liable, in our retirement, to wandering thoughts; and I doubt not, that hours have been wasted in the closet in a vain attempt to fix the mind, while it eluded the effort, and sported itself in fanciful and foolish visions.

It is important, therefore, that we at once counteract this desultory state of mind, by fervent prayer to God. We should then, in a measure, anticipate Satan, who is always most busy with the children of God when they are the nearest to duty, and are about to receive some great spiritual benefit.

Our self-examination, I have already said, respects our state of feelings, and our external conduct. Has the former partaken of the spirit of Christ? Has the latter corresponded with his precepts? It is no very difficult matter for a conscientious and reflecting individual to retrace the occurrences of a single day. But if the business be deferred for weeks and months, his sins will be multiplied and forgotten amid the fluctuating scenes of life. Conscious that there has been much, in both heart and life, to condemn, but forgetting the particulars, he is obliged to repent in the gross.

But he who daily calls himself to an account, will, after a few trials, find the employment both easy and edifying. With what feelings, he will ask, did I awake? Did my gratitude for nocturnal repose and protection rise with the rising light to Him who is the Watchman of Israel, and who never slumbereth nor sleepeth? Or was I, like the brute, indifferent to the kindness of my heavenly Guardian? Did I arise with the breath of praise on my lips, and the spirit of devotion in my heart? Or were my thoughts scattered and desultory? In my morning devotions, can I say that I enjoyed a near access to God, so that I communed with him even as it were from the mercy-seat? Did I wrestle? Did I agonize? Was this the spirit, or were my prayers formal and forced? Was my frame of mind sluggish and cold? Were my petitions hurried and insincere? Did I really desire the blessings I sought; or did I only mention

SELF-EXAMINATION. 115

them as a necessary part of prayer? Had I a deep sense of my unworthiness, and a full conviction of the necessity of my Mediator's blood and merits? In my petitions, was my soul drawn forth in solicitude for others; or did I confine them to myself?

Having left my closet, did I watch unto prayer? I besought God to keep me from sin; but has my conduct this day been in unison with my prayers? I prayed for sanctification; but have I detected and suppressed the first risings of secret iniquity? I entreated God for more light and knowledge; but have I meditated on his works, and studied his word? I deprecated my easily besetting sin; but have I endeavored to avoid it? I prayed for Zion, and for the salvation of the impenitent; but have I spoken a word of warning or exhortation to any person this day? Have I watched the leadings of Providence? Have I advanced in the knowledge of God? Have I made any new discoveries of his glory? Have I learned more of the machinations of Satan, or seen deeper into the deceitfulness of my own heart?

These are a few general questions, which may serve as a guide to one who wishes an outline of daily self-examination.

LETTER XIX.

FAITHFUL SELF-EXAMINATION.

In my last communication, I instituted some inquiries, which, as I supposed, would be profitably connected with a retrospect of the day. I am aware, my young friend, that one person cannot lay down rules on this subject which shall apply precisely to the feelings and circumstances of others. I give you, therefore, only a sketch, by which your inexperience may possibly be benefited.

The questions which one would wish to propose, in taking a retrospect of the day, must of course vary according to circumstances.

I, who am a minister, and who have the care of souls, must inquire more particularly into my fidelity. Have I wrestled this day for the souls of my dear people? Have I improved every opportunity to do them good? Have I preached the truth as it is in Jesus? etc.

But you, in inquiring into your conduct, must adapt those inquiries to the circumstances by which *you* are surrounded. You have personal and relative duties, which are peculiar. Parental esteem and obedience are obligatory. How, you should inquire, have I conducted towards my dear parents this day?

Have I alleviated any of their cares? Have I been obedient and affectionate? I have sisters; have I done my duty towards them, instructing them, and exhibiting an example which they might with safety follow? I am surrounded by companions, some of whom profess the same hopes as myself, but others are yet in "the gall of bitterness and the bonds of iniquity;" have I, so far as opportunity would permit, encouraged the former, and warned the latter? What studies have I pursued, or what books perused? What benefit have I derived from either? Have I done any thing this day for the glory of God? These are some of the questions which I should suppose would occur to one in your circumstances.

If, upon such a daily review, you find that you have advanced in holiness; that you have gained an advantage over your spiritual enemies; that you have profited by the means which a kind Providence has given for your improvement, it will afford matter for praise and thanksgiving. It will kindle up a lively gratitude in your soul, and give a zest to your devotions. If you discover much to condemn, many sins and failures, as you undoubtedly will, it will afford subject for humiliation, and prostrate the soul in penitential confession before God. Thus, while you advance in the knowledge of your own heart, you will have all the ingredients of acceptable worship. Your prayer will be full of praise, and full of contrition.

Your mercies will call forth the one, and your transgressions prompt the other. Prayer with you will then be, not a cold formality, but a deep spiritual intercourse with God and your own heart.

This nocturnal ordeal will bring into view and make precious the merits and intercession of Jesus, your High-priest and Saviour. A review, even of a single day, must, if it be close and careful, ever cover you with confusion of face. The sins committed, even in that short period, will appear numerous. The soul would sink under their heavy load, were it not for the encouraging promise, "If any man sin, we have an advocate with the Father, Jesus Christ the righteous." As sins appear numerous and aggravated, Jesus must ever appear proportionably precious. You will cast yourself all guilty in his arms, and find that "though sin has abounded, grace doth much more abound." After such a review as I have recommended, will a new application be made, and a new pardon supplicated from the hand of the Saviour. He will thus be brought constantly in view, and made increasingly dear and delightful.

You see, then, how many and great are the advantages connected with frequent and close self-examination. Can you then live without it a single day? Are you not resolved that, under all ordinary circumstances, it shall be entered upon and performed with as much punctuality as prayer and the reading

SELF-EXAMINATION. 119

of the word of God? I am persuaded, that after what has been said, you will by no means omit it. I think you must perceive, too, that the difficulties, though great, may, by the plan which I propose, be all surmounted. They arise, as I have before observed, from neglect. Days, weeks, and months roll away, and the soul, immersed in the busy cares of life, contracts a defilement, and collects a rubbish, which a momentary and hurried examination may render visible, but can never remove.

The soul of the delinquent is neglected—shamefully neglected. He deserves to have his hope obscured, his faith weakened, his doubts increased. He may be left amid these perplexities, until he is suddenly called to a death-bed, and compelled to take a direct look at his case. It is then a fearful scene. Clouds and darkness curtain his dying pillow; anguish insupportable heaves his dubious bosom. There is no clear sunshine upon his soul; but he lies on the fluctuating wave, uncertain whether he shall outride the beating storm.

Would you avoid such a scene? O yes, I know you would. Then know yourself, ere it arrive. Be faithfully and intimately acquainted with your own heart. Then shall your life be happy and useful, and your death serene, perhaps gloriously triumphant. May you live the life, and die the death of the righteous.

LETTER XX.

SEASONS OF SELF-EXAMINATION.

As an important auxiliary means of advancing in holiness, I would recommend, in addition to this daily self-examination, an attention to the same duty *at stated and peculiar seasons;* such, for example, as the commencement of a new year, the recurrence of your birthday, or when about to enter upon some important change in life. By perusing the biography of those saints who have been most distinguished for exalted piety, you will find that they never permitted such periods to pass by unobserved or unimproved.

There is something in the periodical revolution of the seasons which cannot fail to strike with seriousness a reflecting mind. A single day is of vast importance. When passed, it can never be recalled. With all its cares, its pleasures, and its pains, it has sunk into eternity. It has gone to give tidings of moral conduct, which will be faithfully recorded against the great day of account. Who, then, but the most infatuated, will dare to murder its hours amidst festivity and mirth, when those hours are so fleeting, and so pregnant with eternal results? If a day is so important, a week, a month, or a year, proportionably increases in value, and forms a period in which much may be done, either to grieve the Spirit of God and effect the ruin of the soul, or to promote the cause of our Redeemer, and secure to ourselves an inheritance in the kingdom of glory.

I trust you will, at least annually, review your diary. As one year rolls away, and another succeeds, look back upon the past, and forward to the future. If you have been daily in the habit of self-examination, this will be not a difficult, but an easy task, replete with spiritual benefit. As you retrace the events of the year, the blessings which you have received will inspire you with affectionate confidence and adoring gratitude; and the evils of heart and of life which have marked that period, will fill your soul with penitential sorrow; and like David, prostrate in the dust of humiliation, you will be constrained to sing both of mercy and of judgment.

What have I done, during the past year, to advance the glory of my Redeemer's kingdom? Have I done all that my means and circumstances would allow? What victories have I obtained over myself? Is my easily besetting sin laid aside, or does it too often master my strongest resolutions? Have I a deeper and more intimate communion with God than when the year commenced? Are my desires for holiness stronger? Have I made any apparent advances towards that elevation at which I profess to aim? Are my devotions colder and more infrequent?

Do my sins oftener prevail, and is the world gaining on my esteem and my attention?

These, my young friend, are some of the questions which the observance of such a season would prompt. Let them be seriously met, and sincerely answered. Let a day, if practicable, be specially appropriated to the duty, and let it be accompanied by fasting and prayer.

The time would fail me to enumerate all the advantages, and exhibit the full importance of such periodical investigations. Enter upon them with diligence, and prosecute them with fidelity, and you will find by your own happy experience, that self-examination is not only an important, but a delightful duty.

Your experience and your careful observance of the past, will enable you to calculate for the future. Against the temptations which have proved most successful, you can place a double guard. The circumstances in which you have found yourself peculiarly exposed, you can avoid. The means which have proved most efficacious for your good, and the individuals whose counsels have stimulated you to duty, will be noted; and in future the former will be oftener resorted to, and the latter drawn into more constant and intimate communion.

Your birthday ought also to be improved. I know that many spend that day in festivity and merriment. They deem it an occasion for mirth and hilarity.

Herod made a royal banquet, and assembling all the wealth and beauty of the kingdom, celebrated his birthday with music and dancing. Many, with more circumscribed means, and on a smaller scale, imitate his example. But is there any thing in our birthday to demand such a parade of folly? Is it a matter of mirth and rejoicing, that another year of our short lives has forever gone? Should we celebrate our own speedy career to God's judgment-bar with music and the dance? And especially, if the soul be unreconciled to God, should we chant a jubilee over its approximation to hell?

If any have reason to rejoice, it is the Christian. He is one year nearer his eternal and happy home. But he views himself as so deficient, and his work on earth as so momentous, that he is far from wishing to spend his birthday in festivity. With him it should be a day of serious examination and humiliation. It should be consecrated to God, and the prosperity of the soul.

I hope that you will observe it in this manner, and then it will be a sort of spiritual landmark, to which you can recur amid the tumultuous sea of life; and when your days are numbered on earth, you will be found to have spent them in " wisdom's ways, which are ways of pleasantness ;" and you will look back upon life, though with deep humility, yet without any heart-rending regret.

LETTER XXI.

PREPARATION FOR THE LORD'S SUPPER.

There are so many excellent works on the preparation of the heart necessary to *an acceptable approach to the Lord's supper*, that I shall do little more than to refer you to them. The only objection which I have ever felt to the use of such treatises is, that by their prolixity, and by the numerous items which they have recommended, I have been confused, and sometimes discouraged, in the work of self-examination. If some of them were greatly abridged, and were disencumbered of a multitude of particulars, which it is impossible to carry in the memory, they would, in my opinion, be far more useful. Still, my young friend, I would habitually consult them. They are written, generally, by men of the deepest and most fervent piety, who have not taken those superficial views of church communion, which, among many, are so prevalent. Where they are derived directly from the clear testimony of Scripture, they will save you much trouble in collating the passages which apply more immediately to the subject in hand.

After all, the word of God is the only true standard; and to one who is familiar with the sacred volume, it will not be an irksome task to select the passages which he deems applicable to the work of self-examination. For my own part, I have ever found it attended with the greatest satisfaction, to go directly to the fountainhead. Take the Bible in your hand, and pore over it with an intention to sift your evidences of Christian character. Accompany that perusal with fervent applications to God for light and knowledge; and you will experience a degree of satisfaction which no other mode can afford.

Esteem the sacramental season as one of your most precious privileges. It is then that you are invited to sup at the royal banquet. You have a place at the King's table, and it becomes you to array the soul in the beauties of holiness. Were you invited to the table of some earthly monarch, how eagerly would you anticipate the honor, and what solicitude would you feel, that your apparel might be appropriate, and your conduct correct. But what is this honor, compared with that of sitting at the table of your Lord? See, then, that you are adorned with the wedding-garment. Anticipate an audience with your King, and rush not into his presence with the carelessness of one who goes only to an ordinary meal.

I would not array that sacred table with terrors to your mind. I am convinced that many throw around the hallowed elements a dread solemnity, which makes the timid and faltering believer feel, that if *he*, if one so vile as *he* should touch them, he would eat and drink damnation to himself, and seal for ever his hopelessness and his ruin. It was never the intention of our Lord to hold up such fearful views of this feast of love. There is every thing about it that is inviting. It is a most pathetic appeal to the fearful and troubled soul. It woos in silent, but eloquent terms, the weary and heavy-laden to come and find rest. It is not Sinai, but Calvary. It is not the smoke, or the lightning, or the thunder—no, weak and mourning believer, it is the uplifted cross, and the expiring victim, whose blood speaks peace from every vein. Look on those significant, simple memorials—is there any terror in this scene? Is it not all peace, and love, and mercy to the penitent?

The ordinance of the supper is a memorial of the love and compassion of Christ, a lively emblem of his sufferings for sin. It is a public acknowledgment of our attachment to his cause. Having seriously and sincerely examined ourselves, and finding that we can humbly claim the characteristics of the true disciple, we may come to this feast of love, and commune with our Lord, and with one another, in a composed and humble frame of mind. If our greatest burden is sin, and our only ground of confidence is the Saviour, we have nothing to fear, but every thing to hope from this delightful and affecting ordinance. Much of the profit of partaking of this ordinance, you will recollect, depends on your fidelity in the work of self-examination. If that be neglected, you have no reason to look for a blessing. If it be performed in a hurried and superficial manner, you need not expect much enjoyment in the ordinance. God will be glorified in them that make so near an approach to the mercy-seat.

When you approach the table, I would recommend it to you to simplify your views as much as possible. By endeavoring to think of many things, the mind becomes confused. Having lifted your soul to God for light and feeling, look on the elements, and endeavor to view them as the appropriate memorials of your bleeding Lord. What do you see in that broken bread? Is it not the emblem of the mangled body of the Lamb of God? What meaneth that flowing wine? Is it not the emblem of his blood, which was shed for the remission of sins? And wherefore was that body broken, and that blood poured forth? O, my soul, let thy guilt and transgressions answer. Without the shedding of that blood, there had been no remission. What, then, can I render to my Lord, for all this dying love? I am speechless in gratitude. Here, blessed Saviour, I give thee all I have—this broken, contrite heart Take it, O take it as thine own, wash it in thy blood, and seal it for thyself.

LETTER XXII.

THE SCRIPTURES.

On the subject of prayer and habitual self-examination, I shall add no more. You recollect that I connected with these, as of equal importance, a close and diligent PERUSAL OF THE SCRIPTURES. I shall therefore occupy your attention, for a short time, on this last-mentioned topic.

The importance of making the word of God a devotional study, is evident both from the testimony of that word, and the experience of all eminent saints who have ever lived. The more I study the sacred volume, the more deeply am I impressed with its intrinsic grandeur, and its high importance to me as an accountable creature. Were I banished to a more lonely rock than that inhabited by the Corsican exile, with my Bible I should never want food for the soul, nor a stimulant to the understanding. I am astonished that men of literature, of mere worldly wisdom, do not more frequently drink at this celestial fountain. Were they once to sip at this clear, pure stream, they could not but relish it. The desire to drink, and the relish, however, the Spirit alone can give.

It has charms, as a mere literary production, which

the veriest infidels have been constrained to acknowledge. Prejudice, not long since, had shut out these heavenly stores from many highly cultivated minds. The Bible was so common a book, and was so frequently found in the hands of the poor and the illiterate, that those who claimed to be learned and philosophic, took the liberty to despise it, and thus excluded themselves from the noblest source of mental and moral refinement. A young man of irreligious character, who was a member of a respectable college, on hearing one of the professors allude to the beautiful comparison of our Saviour, when enjoining confidence in the providence of God, " Consider the lilies of the field, how they grow : they toil not, neither do they spin ; and yet I say unto you, that even Solomon, in all his glory, was not arrayed like one of these," turned to a fellow-student, and inquired where that striking and elegant language was found. On learning that it was found in the Bible, he was astonished. Have you never read your Bible ? was the inquiry of his companion. " My Shakspeare," said he, " is all the Bible I ever read." This, I acknowledge, is an extreme case, but there are many analogous to it.

Dr. Franklin, it is said, was once in the company of several ladies of the English nobility, when the conversation turned on pastoral poetry, in which the ladies took a conspicuous part. After hearing their criticisms on various authors, he proposed to read the translation of a pastoral, for their amusement. He read, with a few verbal alterations, the book of Ruth. They were enraptured with the pastoral, and pronounced it the finest they had ever seen in any language. The doctor then gravely told them that he had read it from the Bible. Whether these ladies were professed infidels, or had considered the Scriptures beneath their notice, I am unable to say. I cannot even vouch for the truth of the anecdote. I am persuaded, however, that an occurrence of that nature might have happened daily, at a time when infidelity was in vogue, and the Bible ridiculed and despised. Even in our day, how little attention do the sacred oracles command.

While the shelf groans with elegant literature, and the mind revels amid the flowery fields of Johnson, Addison, and Shakspeare, or the later and more fascinating groves of Sir Walter Scott—the sublimities of the pentateuch and the prophecies; the tender, touching, simple narrations of Christ; the sublime devotional strains of "Israel's king;" the wisdom of the wisest man who ever lived; are regarded as dry and uninteresting. I cannot allow that man or woman to possess even a cultivated or discriminating taste, who thus judges. I have read Homer and Milton; but when I compare their poetry to the lofty strains of David, Habakkuk, and Isaiah, it is the flickering light of a taper to the corruscations of a thunder-cloud, or to the full-orbed splendors of a noonday sun. I have read the pathetic story of Sterne on the incarcerated criminal, and the melting appeal which Sir Walter puts into the mouth of a favorite heroine, when pleading in the royal presence for the life of her sister; but they are tame when compared with the struggling emotions of a Joseph, and the short but heart-rending plea of his brother Judah.

But this comparison might be extended to the various departments of Bible literature. Its moral precepts, how concise, and yet how comprehensive. Its narrations seize on the most prominent and striking circumstances, without including any extraneous or unnecessary matter; and throughout, from Genesis to Revelation, there is an unearthly something which stamps it as intelligence from the·skies. Its analysis of character is wonderful. There is no other book on earth in which there is so accurate, and full, and clear an exhibition of human nature.

But why am I lauding the Bible as a literary composition, to one who views this as its least attractive feature? Why have I digressed from the great point of urging to an elevated standard of piety? Let us return, and view it as the great means of sanctification. "Sanctify them through thy truth," said our blessed Lord; "thy word is truth." This is the charm which so much attracts the pious heart. That heart is not insensible to the elegance of scriptural style, nor indifferent to its bold and beautiful imagery ; but these are not the principal attractions. It is the word of God. It convinces of sin. It stimulates to duty. It rouses from sluggishness. It warns against danger. It unfolds the character of God. It reveals the way of salvation. It delineates the providence of God. It presents the Lamb of God slain for our transgressions. It communicates sweet strains of spiritual devotion. It brings into view a bright and eternal reward. It discloses the wounds of our nature, and offers the healing balm. In short, it embodies all that a Christian in this pilgrimage can need. It is his only chart through this tempestuous life. In trouble, it is his consolation ; in prosperity, his monitor ; in difficulty, his guide. Amid the darkness of death, and while descending into the shadowy valley, it is the day-star that illuminates his path, makes his dying eye bright with hope, and cheers his soul with the prospect of immortal glory.

Is this the book that vain and foolish minds undervalue and despise ? From their folly, my young friend, learn thou a lesson of wisdom. Let your language be,

> "May this blest volume ever lie
> Close to my heart, and near mine eye:
> Till life's last hour my soul engage,
> And be my chosen heritage."

LETTER XXIII.

THE SCRIPTURES—CONTINUED.

I wish you never to forget that the attainment of an elevated standard of piety is intimately connected with an assiduous and diligent perusal of the Scriptures. It is customary to recommend to the young Christian various authors on practical piety. Such authors I cordially unite in recommending; but I fear that the youthful Christian, by too great an attention to *desultory reading*, has sometimes given less attention to the Bible than its paramount importance demands.

Christians, in recommending such books, have taken it for granted that the Bible is diligently and closely studied; but they have taken too much for granted. A taste for religious novelties has been excited, and the precious word has at length become comparatively uninteresting. If any book of mere human composition, be it ever so instructive, is to command more of our interest and attention than the Bible, we should, like Martyn, throw it aside, and reperuse the sacred volume, until we give it, in our hearts, its legitimate prominence and superiority.

When young Christians become devoted to this religious literature, the Bible is very apt to be neglected. They acquire a flippancy in discussing the superficial parts of Christianity; but I insist upon it, that they do not, by such reading, form a sound, consistent, and deeply spiritual character. Far be it from me to undervalue such reading. But I wish to impress upon your mind the superiority of God's word. Other books of a religious character should be considered as subordinate to the Bible. When they throw light upon the sacred volume; when they drive you back to this great fountain of truth; when they quicken your diligence in studying it, and serve rather as handmaids than as rivals, they may be perused with propriety and with profit. But if you find that they draw away your interest from the word of God, and excite a taste for novelties, you must suspect them as rivals, and immediately give again your highest affections to that precious book to which they legitimately belong.

This caution is the more needful, because the press at the present day teems with periodicals and works of fiction, which, bearing a slightly religious aspect, are considered as good substitutes for similar but irreligious books, and are therefore recommended to those whose consciences might revolt at the latter cast of productions. This furnishes a strong temptation to young Christians. I warn them against it. I would not circumscribe their reading entirely to the word of God. I would be far from proscribing any merely innocent or instructive book. Let them drink at the waters of Helicon and Parnassus. Let them be acquainted with poetry, history, and the various excellent works of taste; but I would guard against making this reading paramount to the Bible. I believe there never can be an exalted Christian character, where the Bible is not made the first, and the best, and the most interesting of books. That person who cannot lay aside any volume, however interesting, for the Bible, and who cannot find in the latter a greater relish than in the former, has never attained to an elevated standard of piety.

It has been said, that every thing in a minister's studies should have a reference to the word of God. Through whatever fields of science or of literature he may rove, he should come back with superior relish to the Bible. The same advice should be given to the young Christian. In the varied regions of philosophy and taste he is permitted to rove, but the Bible should be his richest banquet. Make it a rule always to prefer it. If at the hours of devotion you are strongly drawn towards some new and interesting religious publication; if you are tempted to omit for this the regular study of the Scriptures, regard it as a temptation, and resist it accordingly. You recollect the resolution of the pious Martyn, to which I have alluded. He never would allow himself to peruse a book one moment after he felt it gaining a preference to his Bible. As long as he could turn to his Bible with a superior relish, so long he would continue reading, and no longer. Go thou and do likewise. If you commence with this resolution, you will find the advantages of it in your daily experience. The word of God will grow constantly in your estimation, and you will be ready to exclaim with David, "O how I love thy law; it is sweeter to my taste than honey and the honey-comb."

My own experience convinces me, that the oftener and the more diligently you peruse the Scriptures, the more beautiful will they appear, and the less relish will you have for light and superficial reading. There is, in an intimate acquaintance, in a daily conversation with the Scriptures, something sanctifying, something ennobling. A satisfaction is felt in perusing them, which no human composition can excite. You feel as if you were conversing with God and angels. You breathe a heavenly atmosphere. The soul is bathed in celestial waters. It imbibes a sweetness and a composure which shed over it unearthly attractions.

To this fountain of light and life let us then daily resort. Here is the healing influence. Here is the pool of Bethesda. Here abounds consolation for the afflicted. Here hope dwells to cheer and to guide. "Bind this precious volume about your neck; write it on the tablets of your heart." It will prove your shield in conflict, your guide in perplexity, your solace in adversity. When "death shall be swallowed up in victory," if it have been faithfully studied in this life, it will afford themes for heavenly contemplation through eternity.

LETTER XXIV.

STUDY OF THE SCRIPTURES.

It is a common practice with young Christians to confine their attention to certain parts of the Scriptures, to the almost entire neglect of the rest. They select, generally, the devotional and preceptive portions, such as the evangelists, the Psalms, and some of the epistles. This circumstance, while it favors the evidence of their being Christians, is also best calculated, perhaps, to advance their growth in grace. In this early stage of their progress, they cannot be expected to take a comprehensive view of scriptural truth, and exhibit a maturity of knowledge on doctrinal theology. But there is danger that this practice will be too long continued. If so, they will ever be children. They cannot grow in knowledge. They will be feeding on milk when they ought to receive the more substantial aliment.

Permit me, therefore, my young friend, to caution you against undervaluing any part of the inspired volume. While I would rejoice in the fact of your having at first preferred those scriptures which are more particularly devotional, I must exhort you to go on to perfection. "All Scripture is given by inspiration of God," and all is, therefore, profitable for the attainment of that perfect standard at which you aim.

In these remarks I speak from personal experience. My attention, for a long time, was confined almost exclusively to the Psalms, the evangelists, and a few of the plainest of the epistles. These I perused and reperused, until much of them was committed to memory, and all were very familiar. I do not, nor shall I ever regret this. But my mistake was, in supposing that the historical and prophetical, and some of the doctrinal parts of the Bible, were inapplicable to my circumstances, and therefore had little claim on my attention. I fear that others have fallen into this mistake. I have since learned that those very scriptures, to which I confined my attention, were greatly elucidated and beautifully explained by other parts of the Bible, which I had thought too deep and too inapplicable for my reading.

The word of God is one magnificent whole. There is a symmetry in all its proportions, and a harmonious admeasurement in all its parts. It is like a beautiful edifice, constructed on the finest principles of architecture. The young Christian may be compared to a superficial observer, who is enraptured with a glance of the finely turned arches, and the highly finished columns of this temple. He dwells upon these as the principal attractions. The more advanced saint has not only entered the vestibule, but has also penetrated the interior court. He has examined carefully the foundation, and admired its adamantine structure. He has surveyed its halls and its galleries, and has been struck with the beauty of their proportions. He has threaded every labyrinth, and ascertained its direction and its utility. He has found no part defective; no portion superfluous. As his mind sweeps in the noble pile at one glance, he exclaims, How magnificent, how grand, how worthy of the architect!

While, therefore, my young friend, I would encourage you in perusing closely those parts of the Bible which appear most adapted to your character and circumstances, I would at the same time caution you not to neglect other important parts of sacred Scripture. As I before observed, by reading the Bible as a whole, you will perceive much more clearly the beauty of your favorite passages. The true method of interpreting Scripture is by comparing one part with another. Had I received and attended to this hint, my knowledge of scriptural truth would, I am persuaded, have been much more extensive than it is at present. I have learned from happy, though late experience, that the historical books of the Old Testament not only throw light on all the subsequent inspired writings, but are replete with most exalted, and devotional, and soul-transporting sentiments. Since I began to study the

Scriptures in course, I have lingered on the pentateuch as on enchanted ground. The types and shadows have been full of meaning. In all of them, Christ and him crucified appears conspicuous.

I am convinced of the utility of studying the Bible in course; and I can assure you, that my former desultory practice, of opening and reading where the eye chanced to fall, was far from affording equal satisfaction. I note for your benefit the circumstances which prevented my improvement in the knowledge of God's word, and I hope that you will carefully avoid them. You will find a solid satisfaction in studying the Scriptures according to the mode I recommend. Consider it as the labor of life; for be assured, that should you live to the age of fourscore years, you will not have attained perfection in this study. But why should I call it a labor, when it is so delightful a privilege? It is indeed a labor to that being who loves not the character, and who yields not obedience to the law of God. But is it a labor to that mind which is attuned, by the Spirit's influence, to the beauties of celestial truth? Will not the soul expand under the developments of God, and of heavenly things?

As we learn more and more of the wisdom, the goodness, and the mercy of God, we shall the more ardently desire a conformity to these divine attributes. It is thus we shall grow in grace, and in the knowledge of God, and of our Saviour. In the visible creation, every thing is full of glory. Every thing speaks of the wisdom and the power of God, and invites the soul to ascend to its all-glorious Creator. But in the written word, we have God speaking to us without a medium, and speaking to us as to his children.

Go, then, my young friend, and diligently listen to the holy oracles. Search the Scriptures. Peruse them systematically. Make them your daily and nightly companions. And may their celestial influence be so infused into your soul, that you shall progressively lose the image of the earthly, and assume the image of the heavenly inhabitants.

LETTER XXV.

STUDY OF THE SCRIPTURES.

You recollect, my young friend, that when speaking on the subject of prayer, I warned you against a hurried and superficial manner. I would repeat the same caution in respect to reading the word of God. There is a careless, superficial attention to the Bible, which is neither acceptable to God, nor profitable to the soul.

We should ever approach that sacred book with reverence. Though written by men, remember that those men "spake as they were moved by the Holy Spirit." The medium through which it was communicated, detracts not from the divinity of the matter. When we open the sacred volume, we listen to the voice of God. It is the same voice, though unaccompanied by those terrific circumstances, which issued from that awful cloud which curtained the summit of Sinai. It is the same voice that was heard in such piteous lamentations from Calvary, when our Immanuel trode for us the wine-press of the wrath of God. Should we not, therefore, give a reverential attention when Jehovah speaks? Should not our posture be that of the deepest humility and awe?

When you take the Scriptures in hand, it is well to let such a reflection pass your mind. It is profitable to pause a moment, and say within yourself, What a privilege do I enjoy in the perusal of this sacred page. Millions of my fellow-beings are shut out from it. They have nothing but the dim and flickering light of nature. They are, therefore, degraded and besotted by ignorance and sensuality. Whereas I am favored with the clear light of revelation. I hold in my hand the mind and will of God concerning me. Are not my obligations, therefore, proportionably great? What account can I give at the judgment-day, if I neglect or undervalue this precious volume? "O Lord, open thou mine eyes, that I may behold wondrous things out of thy law." Unstop mine ear, that I may listen, and dispose my heart to receive and obey. Spirit of light, Inspirer of this heavenly book, be present to dissipate my darkness, and shed over my soul the beams of celestial glory. Let me not fall under the condemnation of that wicked servant, who knew his master's will, but refused to perform it; but having, by thy illuminating influence, a perfect understanding of the word, may I, through thy sanctifying grace, be moulded by it into the likeness and image of God.

I take it for granted, that the study of the Bible is to form a part of your daily devotions; and it is upon such a supposition that I make these remarks. Beware, I entreat you, of the habit of glancing over different parts of the Bible, instead of perusing it in course, and with close and diligent attention. The latter mode, accompanied with the blessing of God, will form an elevated Christian character. The former is characteristic of the worldly-minded and superficial professor. Depend upon it, the closer attention you give to the word, the more precious and interesting will it become, and the more rapidly will you grow in knowledge and holiness. The pious David declared that his love for the word of God was so ardent, that it was his meditation day and night. I meditate, says he, on all thy precepts. I muse on the work of thy hands. It is this meditative spirit which I would recommend, when you are perusing the Scriptures.

The celebrated Dr. Scott, as we learn from his memoirs, was in the habit of reading the Bible on his knees. Whenever a difficult part of divine truth came under consideration, he would lift his soul to God for the illuminating influence of the Spirit. It was by prayer over the word of God, that this eminent saint formed a character that will stand as a bright example to all succeeding Christians. It was in this way, also, that he arrived at such a profound knowledge of the Scriptures, and was enabled to write his celebrated commentary. As you will need some helps in studying the Bible, permit me, without claiming that any human author is free from error, to recommend this invaluable work as among the best commentaries extant.

I cannot do this better, than by copying a brief notice from the pen of a clerical friend. "I have never met with a commentator so admirably adapted to ordinary use as Dr. Scott. As an interpreter, he is clear, sober, and judicious. He never so dwells upon one doctrine as to keep others out of view—the grand defect of many expositors—but gives to each truth that proportion of notice which its relative importance seems to demand. The great doctrine of justification by faith alone, the very hinge on which the whole Gospel turns, and its all-pervading principle, Dr. Scott very clearly and fully unfolds, where it is specially treated of in holy writ. He never loses sight of it upon any occasion, and uniformly so handles it, as to beat down the pride of the pharisee on the one hand, and expose the rottenness of the antinomian on the other. But his commentary is not simply doctrinal; he shows all the varied bearings of the truth upon the inner and the outer man. In a word, he is highly experimental and practical throughout. And for this part of his work, he appears peculiarly competent. Never, perhaps, were displayed in any uninspired composition, such a deep insight into the natural workings of the human heart, and so accurate a knowledge of the exercises of a mind renewed by divine grace, combined with such an enlarged, and at the same time minute acquaintance with human life, under every variety of circumstance. To write this work, demanded such observation of the world, united to such studious habits, as could very rarely indeed be found in the same individual. And the Lord seems to have led this wonderful man through just the path that would qualify him to compose such a book."

I can add my testimony to the above. Although I had frequently heard Dr. Scott undervalued, as not sufficiently critical, I am now convinced that he has been wise in not encumbering his work with useless criticism, which, while it might have pleased the few, would have been a great disadvantage to the many. It will be found, I believe, that his opinion on all the great practical truths and doctrines of the Bible, is the correct one. I must conclude, therefore, by advising you to commence his work with a determination, by the blessing of God, to finish it. Prospectively, it may appear a herculean task; but be assured, it is not. As you advance, you will find each succeeding page more and more delightful.

LETTER XXVI.
STUDY OF THE SCRIPTURES.

I HOPE, my young friend, that you will acquire a thorough acquaintance with *the historical* scriptures. They are intimately connected with the prophetical, the doctrinal, and the preceptive parts of the Bible. I have at times been made to blush for my ignorance of some fact which has been alluded to as a part of Bible history, and especially as quoted by the New Testament writers; not because I neglected the Bible, but because I confined my reading to a very limited portion of it.

It is impossible to understand the prophecies, without a knowledge of the sacred history. It is equally impossible, without this knowledge, to comprehend the beauty and force of the gospels and the epistles. The more thoroughly you study the Old, the more easily will you comprehend the meaning and beauty of the New Testament. If you will become intimately acquainted with the book of Leviticus, the epistle to the Hebrews will possess charms which you had never attributed to it. If you have discriminated between the covenant which God made with Abraham, and that which he formed with the people of Israel at Sinai, you will be prepared to estimate the force of the apostle's reasoning in the epistle to the Galatians. There is scarcely any part of the New Testament which has not some connection with the Old. In the historical books, you have also an exhibition of the providence of God, and many bright examples of patriarchal Christianity. You cannot fail, therefore, of being amply rewarded by a diligent perusal of the sacred history.

In studying the *doctrinal* parts of the Bible, you will require much patience and perseverance, mingled with constant prayer for heavenly illumination. There is reason to apprehend that many young Christians have vague and superficial notions of the doctrines, whilst they exhibit much of the true temper of the Gospel. If, however, they neglect to investigate and understand the doctrines of Scripture, they will be in danger of being led astray by the seducing influence of heresy. Be well grounded, therefore, in the fundamental doctrines of the Bible. In making up your opinion with respect to any doctrine, avoid a rash and hasty conclusion. Be deliberate, and you will escape the imputation of "being carried about with every wind of doctrine." When a truth which you have thus deliberately embraced is called in question, be not induced by the apparent candor, or the plausible arguments of your opponent, to yield your opinion, until you have given it a thorough investigation. You may still be right, and your opponent wrong. Be not rash in giving up *your* opinion and adopting *his.* This caution is perhaps necessary to young Christians, who cannot at their age be supposed to be thoroughly indoctrinated.

The great truths of evangelical religion you have received from education. I would advise you to re-examine them by the word of God, and if they correspond therewith, to hold them fast, as the most precious legacy which your pious parents have bequeathed. It will be insinuated, perhaps, that such opinions are the result of education, and are destitute of any other foundation. Be cautious in admitting this. Search the Scriptures, and if you find them there, hold them fast, as a " form of sound words." If they were opposed to the Bible, you ought to abandon them, however dear, or sanctified by parental affection. But in yielding such opinions, I would still say, be not rash. Investigate closely and candidly, ere you let them go. There is a tenderness of conscience in young Christians, which Satan sometimes pushes to a painful and distressing embarrassment. This is as much the case in respect to belief, as to external conduct.

As an illustration of these remarks, there occurs to my recollection the case of a youth, who, on making a public profession of religion, joined, as a matter of course, the church to which his parents belonged. For a short time all went happily with him. He enjoyed the communion of the saints, and the ordinances of the Gospel. The scene, however, was soon changed. His mind was thrown into great distress by the insinuations of one, who, by his bold and dogmatical mode of reasoning, led him into doubts on a particular point of doctrine. He was deeply perplexed as to the path of duty. At one time, the adversary would suggest the guilt of remaining a day longer in his present connection. At another, he would insinuate that he had made a false profession, and therefore had committed the sin against the Holy Ghost. In this hour of anguish, he prayed most earnestly for direction. The thought occurred to him, that he need not be rash in altering his views. As he was comparatively a child, and had much to learn, God would not be displeased if he took time for investigation. This thought gave him consolation, and he set about a diligent and prayerful examination of his Bible. The result was, a conviction of the truth as he had held it, and a perfectly settled state of mind on that point, even to the present time.

I hope, therefore, my young friend, that in making up your doctrinal opinions, you will study the word of God closely and prayerfully. Be careful not to rush into hasty conclusions from isolated passages; but take a comprehensive view of the connection. Look at the Bible in all its grand and magnificent proportions. Be thoroughly indoctrinated, and you will become a growing and stable Christian. There will be a solidity in your character, which, like a foundation that is well adjusted to the superstructure, will be at once the evidence both of permanency and of beauty.

LETTER XXVII.

STUDY OF THE SCRIPTURES.

I would not, my young friend, have you study the Bible *as a critic*, but as a Christian. You should endeavor to derive some spiritual nourishment from every part of Scripture. In this, Dr. Scott's commentary is admirably calculated to assist you. In studying the historical Scriptures, you can occasionally pause and meditate. You can inquire whether your mind distinctly comprehended the facts recorded, and their practical bearing. In this way, your memory will be strengthened, and your heart, I trust, often affected.

Before I leave this subject, permit me to say a word or two on the spirit with which you should peruse the sacred volume. It is a spirit of implicit faith, and childlike docility. There are many parts of Scripture, which, after the most diligent and careful investigation, will still appear, to short-sighted man, almost inexplicable. There are many doctrines too profound for human comprehension—many mysterious truths relating to God, to angels, and to heaven. God has given to man a revelation which embodies the august truths of his eternity, and of his infinite attributes; which brings into view a spiritual world, and throws down upon us the light of the inconceivable glory; and such a revelation must necessarily contain things to us mysterious and incomprehensible. It necessarily presents certain truths to be received on the simple testimony of God; and this is faith. Shall I, therefore, in perusing the Bible, reject one of its doctrines, because it is less intelligible than another? Am I not bound to receive even incomprehensible truths, if I find them there recorded? Having settled the fact that the Bible is inspired, I must come to it as to an infallible oracle. I must feel, with the apostle, that although there are many things which, in consequence of my infirmity, I can only view as through a glass darkly; yet, if I am a Christian, the time is near when I shall see them as clearly as I can behold a friend face to face. Although I must confess that there are many deep truths which now I know but in part, yet there is a day coming when I shall know them as fully as I myself am known. Even the venerable apostle ranks himself but as a child in the knowledge of divine things. He is content to wait until that knowledge shall be expanded among the bright intelligences of heaven.

Were your father, whom you so much love, an astronomer, conversant with the motions of the heavenly bodies—were he to take you, while a child, to his observatory, point you to those revolving orbs, and tell you that he had measured their distances, and calculated their motions, would you believe him? O yes; he is your father, who would not deceive you, and you are his confiding child. You could not comprehend the fact, but you would believe your father; you would have no doubt of his veracity. Were he again to tell you, that should your life be continued, you also would, in a few years, be able to make these sublime calculations, your astonishment would be increased. Had not your father said it, you could not have believed it. But still you would confide in your beloved parent.

This is precisely the spirit which you must possess in studying the Scriptures. It is your Father who speaks. Sometimes he speaks of high and mysterious things; but remember, that you are bound to confide in his word. When scepticism would harass your mind, flee to the word of God, and subject your understanding implicitly to its dictates. When troubles assail, betake yourself instantly to this fountain of consolation. When doubts of your acceptance come over your mind like a dark and portentous cloud, here, in this blessed volume, is the Sun of righteousness to chase away the cloud, and restore you to calmness and tranquillity.

Whilst there is a spirit abroad that would undervalue the plain testimony of revelation, and make it, like the heathen oracles of old, speak an ambiguous and time-serving language, be it your resolution to cling to the precious Bible, and to love even its most self-denying and soul-humbling doctrines. Be not ashamed of those views of truth which, in the estimation of vain and proud man, are peculiar only to vulgar minds. The Bible, you will recollect, was written equally for the vulgar and the refined. The poor claim it as their most precious legacy. What though there be in it some mysterious and inexplicable doctrines; is it not the part of faith to sit meekly at the Saviour's feet, and receive implicitly the words which drop from his lips?

Compassed about as we are with infirmities—dependent as we are for the least ray of heavenly comfort—with intellectual pride on the one hand, and deep-rooted and sinful prejudices on the other—now wandering from God and duty, and now returning disappointed and dejected—let us sink into the deepest self-abasement. Let us bow, with the spirit of children, to the simple truth as it is in Jesus; let us implore the divine Spirit to guide us through this benighted desert; and let us look forward by faith to the period when we shall emerge from our darkness into unclouded and eternal day.

LETTER XXVIII.

RELIGION THE BUSINESS OF LIFE.

By this time, my young friend, you perceive that religion is *the business of life*—a momentous work, which will task every faculty to the utmost. To make a profession in the visible church is one thing; but to evince, by a progressive improvement in knowledge and holiness, our connection with the church invisible, is another. When I look around and behold so many youth gathered within the church by the sanctifying influence of the numerous and powerful revivals of religion, my soul exults in the prospective glories of our Zion. These, methinks, are the generations who are to urge forward the cause of Christ, and who may be permitted to chant the jubilee of millennial glory.

I am anxious that the rising generation of Christians should assume a more elevated standard of piety and action than that which has characterized their predecessors; and that primitive holiness, and magnanimity, and self-denial, should once more appear, as the earnest and pledge of that glorious consummation when holiness shall be inscribed even on the bells of the horses. I confess, however, that I have my misgivings. I have seen some who but lately gave auspicious promise of this high and noble character, sinking down to the dead level of ordinary professors, taking the hue and character of those around them, and appearing contented with just so much religion as will render them agreeable to all, without incurring the censure of any. How unworthy of a great and noble character! I would never name the name of Christ, or I would give him my *heart*—my full, free, undivided heart.

The gospel of Christ admits of no compromise. It demands our all. If it required less, it would be unworthy of its great author and finisher. I rejoice that it requires all. This is its glory. When we are brought to yield to its claims, and give up all, then, and not till then, will it throw around us its arms of mercy. And what *is* our all? What do we give when we give our all? A polluted soul, that might justly be cast into hell; a body, the miserable companion of that soul, and groaning under the dire effects of disobedience and guilt. Our all consists, at last, in nothing more than a polluted and guilty nature.

What a wonder is it that God will accept such an offering. What a miracle of mercy, that raises us up from our pollution, bathes us in the laver of regeneration, and clothes us in the white linen of the saints. And do we talk about self-denial? Do we say, how hard to give up all? I am ashamed to use such language; ashamed to hear it used. What did Christ give up for us? Let that question blot out "self-denial" from the Christian's vocabulary. When you think the Gospel makes severe requisitions by requiring all, go up to Mount Calvary and weep over such suggestions. See the blood of your Immanuel so freely gushing from a heart that never exercised towards you any emotion but love; love unspeakable—love unsought—and love for the guilty. Go hide your head in shame and penitence at such a thought. It is a glorious privilege, my young friend, to give up all to Christ. The soul that feels the constraining influence of his love, asks not how little may be given consistently with obtaining the heavenly reward—asks not for the lowest standard of discipleship; it burns with an ardent desire to devote all, and to aim at perfect " conformity to his death."

It is melancholy to behold so many satisfied with a name in the church, and a seat at the sacramental board. This appears to make up the sum of their religion. Others go one step farther, and observe some decent regard to what may be termed the experimental part of religion, but aim not at that elevated standard which it is their privilege to attain. They live in doubt, and they often die in darkness. They enjoy neither religious consolations nor the peace which the world giveth. All this is in consequence of that miserable, half-way, compromising spirit, which seeks to perform the service, and enjoy the approbation of two masters

Let me entreat you to make a noble surrender in this cause. The world has hitherto been the master, and you must acknowledge that you have rendered a full and faithful service; but shall you yield a less free and faithful devotion to Christ? Which is the more worthy of your regard? Which has the greater claims on your affections? Which offers the fullest reward? Determine, by the grace of God, that you will forsake all, and follow Christ: do not, like Peter, follow him afar off, but, like Mary, sit at his feet— like the beloved disciple, rest upon his bosom.

You will perceive from my communications thus far, that there is work enough to do; that there is some struggling for the prize; that the kingdom of heaven is to be taken by violence; that you are not to sit down and idly imagine, that now you have joined the church, there remaineth no more for you to do; that you are to be carried along, as it were, by a sort of invisible influence to heaven, without any extraordinary exertions of your own. Determine, that if others act on the principles of the spiritual sluggard, you will leave them, and march forward towards the elevation of Christian character which the Bible plainly marks out as your duty and your privilege. Onward, is the daily watchword of the faithful soldier of the cross. He sleeps not at his post. He hears the first note of alarm, and prepares for the conflict. He loves his King, and obedience is a pleasure rather than a duty. Many a bright example still shines in your view. A Brainerd, a Martyn, a Graham, a Judson, and a Newell, have left the light of their glorious career still lingering on earth. Plant your feet in their tracks, and if you cannot equal, at least make a near approximation to them. Dread the thought of being any thing less than they were; and remember, that it is possible even to surpass them.

O may you aim high, in contending for the prize of your high calling. May you go from strength to strength, from victory to victory, from one attainment to another, until you shall stand a glorious example on earth—until you shall inherit the highest rewards of the blessed in heaven.

LETTER XXIX.

RELIGION THE BUSINESS OF LIFE.

The duties which I have been urging upon you, as important in forming an elevated standard of piety, are those especially which relate to God and your own soul. *Social obligations*, and the relative duties of life, I have not considered. They are not first in importance. Besides, if you give heed to the advice which I have presented in these sheets; if you persevere in the path which I have marked out; if you give the diligence in prayer, in self-examination, and the study of the Bible which I have urged, you will, most certainly, not be a delinquent in the various social and domestic duties of life.

The course recommended, if faithfully pursued, will have a controlling influence upon your intercourse with others. It will put every thing in its proper place, and give every duty its legitimate prominency and attention. It will make you the obedient child, the beloved sister, the diligent scholar, and the amiable and intelligent companion. It will render you in every respect lovely and interesting. It is under this impression that I have given to this subject a protracted consideration, and that I have said so little about your general deportment. I have endeavored first to erect the solid column; the Corinthian capital can be easily superadded.

I might have added something more, on the importance of Christian biography as a means of stimulating the young Christian, but I take it for granted that you are already familiar with most of the popular works of that kind, which are now so much read and so justly admired. The memoirs of Brainerd, Pearce, Martyn, and Scott; the lives of Mrs. Graham, Ramsay, Newell, and Huntington, cannot be read too often, nor copied too closely. You will find it highly useful, in your daily retirement, to hold converse with some of these exalted saints. It will furnish a humbling view of your own comparative sluggishness, and arouse you to emulate their noble self-denial and devotion. Next to your Bible, may they be your most intimate and beloved companions.

But ah, how small a number of such characters have ever lived to grace this fallen world. "Like angel visitors, they have been few and far between." They have shot athwart our world, to evidence to scoffers and infidels the genuine beauty of Christianity, and to exhibit for the imitation of their brethren that high and noble character to which human nature, degraded as it is, can, by the spirit and grace of God, be elevated. When I read of their self-denial; their entire consecration of all to the service of Christ; their agonizing prayers, which were offered less for themselves than for the perishing souls around them; their enlarged benevolence, which was satisfied with nothing short of blessing a world; when I consider their patience in suffering, their cheerfulness under repeated and severe afflictions, their composure and triumph in death, I view them as possessing a character which naught but a superhuman power can confer; far, very far transcending the brightest models of Grecian or of Roman virtue. They scarcely seem to belong to our species; and if fancy were permitted to decide, we should almost say, that in them the glory and brightness of some seraph was displayed.

But still, my young friend, "they were bone of our bone, and flesh of our flesh." They possessed, in common with us, the same sickly, sinful nature. They made no pretensions to superiority. Nay, they considered their own characters as vile, in the eyes of Him who "cannot look upon sin." If they possessed an elevation of character above us, they seemed not to know it. They were, while shining out with angel virtue, all meekness and humility. These are the characters which, though undervalued by the world, make their silent progress through life, indifferent to the honors and the pleasures which inferior and sordid minds are struggling to obtain. These are the characters which, while they walk on earth, converse with the skies, hold communion—intimate, deep, delightful communion—with heaven. Their souls daily disentangling themselves from the bonds of sensuality, severing their willing affections from the dross and corruption of earth, rise to a similitude with God; and ere they leave their earthly abode, appear to imbibe a purity and a perfection, which are a sort of earnest of their quick transition to glory.

But my pen is unable to render a just tribute to characters so bright and magnificent. The simple narrative will speak a stronger eulogy.

Such are the characters which I wish you to copy. They are the only happy characters. There is a delightful, yet mournful contrast between them and that cold-hearted, half-devoted, earthly-minded race of professors, who, I verily believe, are among the most miserable beings on earth. They are a disgrace to the Christian church; a standing scandal upon religion; a grief to the pious; a laughing-stock to the world. Over their worldly-mindedness, their niggardly charities, their hollow professions, thousands stumble into perdition. Avoid this character, as you regard the peace of your own soul, the prosperity of the church, the advancement of Christ's kingdom, and your final salvation.

Remember, that there is a day coming when the precious will be separated from the vile, when the

Master shall walk through the Christian church, and "shall gather the wheat into his garner, and burn up the chaff with unquenchable fire." Be not, my young friend, satisfied with grovelling views, or low attainments. Aim high, even at perfection; for you know that a greater than man hath said, "Be ye perfect, as your Father in heaven is perfect."

CONCLUSION.

I CANNOT believe, my young friend, that the serious cautions, solemn warnings, and earnest appeals which I have made, are to be entirely lost. I flatter myself, that when the hand which penned, and the heart which prompted them, are resting in the grave, she, for whose instruction they were given, will exhibit all that maturity of knowledge, all that purity of character, all that holy elevation of purpose and of action, which together constitute the fulness of Christian perfection. But if, after all, you should make a compromise with the world, and be willing to settle down upon that low and unworthy standard too common among our churches—if a few years should find you foremost in pleasure and in fashion, and undistinguished from the noisy, vain, and trifling crowd, methinks your conscience will have been rapidly seared, and your heart quickly steeled to a sense of your duty.

But I am persuaded better things of you, though I thus speak. Still, I know more than you can at present of the deceitfulness of the heart, the subtle insinuations of Satan, and the powerful attractions which the world presents to a warm, youthful imagination. Secluded as you now are, you can form but a faint conception of the power of worldly seductions

Perhaps you are ready to conclude, that your heart is impregnable to all their assaults. This, be assured, is a great mistake. Think not that your mountain stands strong. If you indulge this thought, you will most assuredly fall; you will be obliged to weep over the disgrace which you will have brought upon religion; you will, perhaps, be constrained to bewail the ruin of some soul, who may have been emboldened in sin through your carelessness or inadvertency. You have a dangerous road to travel. You cannot be too vigilant; you cannot offer too many prayers for guidance and protection. Your armor cannot be too bright, nor your eye too circumspect.

Remember what I have already said, that declension begins at the closet. Watch there for its first appearance. There be ready to discover and to correct it. Prayer is your stronghold. In every encounter with your adversaries, draw upon the strength of heaven. In every dark, distressful hour, cast an eye upward to God. When the world displays its fascinations, and woos you away to its arms, God, and God alone, is the "strength of your heart." When afflictions come, and the soul is made sad and desolate, where then shall you look, but to Him who heareth the mourner's cry? Prayer has ever been powerful and efficient. It has wiped away the tear of the penitent, and lighted up the gleam of hope.

It has broken the stout sinews of rebellion, and transformed the lion to the lamb.

In the work of self-examination, be close and thorough—be habitual and persevering. Let a nice discrimination run through your investigations. Remember your aim. It is high; it is the elevated character. Deal faithfully, then, with your own soul. Arraign it at a diurnal tribunal, and judge it, severely judge it, from the law of God. Anticipate the great and final account. It will then not burst upon you unprepared. You will go calmly forward to the bar of God, and unhesitatingly open your bosom, conscious of forgiveness, to his keen inspection.

Let the word of God dwell in your heart. Study its sacred pages with prayerful diligence, and bow to its doctrines with implicit faith. Be it the man of your counsel; the guide of your belief; the foundation of your hope.

In short, take to yourself the whole armor of God: the shield of faith, by which you may quench the fiery darts of Satan; the helmet of salvation, to adorn and defend your head; the breastplate of righteousness, to cover your bosom from the shafts of calumny or of envy; the sword of the Spirit, whose keen edge will make you resolute and fearless in the attack, powerful and irresistible in the defence. Thus arrayed, look upward, and press onward. God is your strength, and when he nerves the arm, though it be the arm of the weakest believer, that arm is irresistible. Lay not aside your weapons, while one foe within is unsubdued, or one enemy without unconquered. But life is short. The time is at hand when you shall have a full and free discharge. The crown of glory glitters in prospect. After a few more days of fidelity to your King, that crown shall be placed upon your brow.

When death comes, he will prove your last enemy. As he falls beneath your triumphant struggle, you shall hear the notes of victory, bursting from ten thousand angels, on your dying ear. Then your work is done. Then your warfare is over. On yonder heavenly plains, you shall receive a golden harp, and learn celestial music. You shall sound that name by which you conquered; and in your eternal song, chant the praise of Him who sitteth upon the throne, and of the Lamb for ever. The trials of life will be remembered no more; or if remembered, will serve as new themes of praise and thanksgiving.

What a consummation! Who would not struggle a few short days, to inherit so rich a reward—to wear forever so bright a diadem?

SGCB Titles for the Young

Solid Ground Christian Books is honored to be able to offer a full dozen uncovered treasure for children and young people.

The Child's Book on the Fall by Thomas H. Gallaudet is a simple and practical exposition of the Fall of man into sin, and his only hope of salvation.

Repentance & Faith: *Explained and Illustrated for the Young* by Charles Walker, is a two in one book introducing children to the difference between true and false faith and repentance.

The Child at Home by John S.C. Abbott is the sequel to his popular book *The Mother at Home*. A must read for children and their parents.

My Brother's Keeper: *Letters to a Younger Brother* by J.W. Alexander contains the actual letters Alexander sent to his ten year old brother.

The Scripture Guide by J.W. Alexander is filled with page after page of information on getting the most from our Bibles. Invaluable!

Feed My Lambs: *Lectures to Children* by John Todd is drawn from actual sermons preached in Philadelphia, PA and Pittsfield, MA to the children of the church, one Sunday each month. A pure gold-mine of instruction.

Heroes of the Reformation by Richard Newton is a unique volume that introduces children and young people to the leading figures and incidents of the Reformation. Spurgeon called him, *"The Prince of preachers to the young."*

Heroes of the Early Church by Richard Newton is the sequel to the above-named volume. The very last book Newton wrote introduces all the leading figures of the early church with lessons to be learned from each figure.

The King's Highway: *Ten Commandments to the Young* by Richard Newton is a volume of Newton's sermons to children. Highly recommended!

The Life of Jesus Christ for the Young by Richard Newton is a double volume set that traces the Gospel from Genesis 3:15 to the Ascension of our Lord and the outpouring of His Spirit on the Day of Pentecost. Excellent!

The Young Lady's Guide by Harvey Newcomb will speak directly to the heart of the young women who desire to serve Christ with all their being.

The Chief End of Man by John Hall is an exposition and application of the first question of the Westminster Shorter Catechism. Full of rich illustrations.

Call us Toll Free at 1-877-666-9469
Send us an e-mail at sgcb@charter.net
Visit us on line at solid-ground-books.com

OTHER SOLID GROUND TITLES

In addition to *Advice to a Young Christian* we are happy to offer the following titles to help equip you to serve our Lord and Savior.

Assurance of Faith by Louis Berkhof
The Backslider: *Nature, Symptoms & Recovery* by Andrew Fuller
My Brother's Keeper: *Letters to a Younger Brother* by J.W. Alexander
The Chief End of Man by John Hall
Church Member's Guide by John Angell James
Come Ye Apart: *Gospel Devotions* by J.R. Miller
Communicant's Companion by Matthew Henry
Divine Love: *Sermons on the Love of the Triune God* by John Eadie
The Doctrine of Justification by James Buchanan
Friendship: *The Master Passion* by H. Clay Trumbull
From the Pulpit to the Palm-Branch: *Memorial to C.H. Spurgeon*
Imago Christi: *The Example of Jesus Christ* by James Stalker
Jesus of Nazareth: *Character, Teaching & Miracles* by J.A. Broadus
The Man of Business by J.W. Alexander, W.B. Sprague and more
Manual for the Young by Charles Bridges
Notes on Galatians by J. Gresham Machen
Opening Scripture: *Hermeneutical Manual* by Patrick Fairbairn
Opening Up Ephesians by Peter Jeffery
Pastor's Sketches: *Case Studies with Troubled Souls* by I.S. Spencer
Pathway into the Psalter by William Binnie
Paul the Preacher: *Studies on Discourses in Acts* by John Eadie
Power of God unto Salvation by Benjamin B. Warfield
Secret of Communion with God by Matthew Henry
The Still Hour: *Communion with God in Prayer* by Austin Phelps
The Transfigured Life: *Selected Shorter Writings of J.R. Miller*
The Travels of True Godliness: *An Allegory* by Benjamin Keach
Whatsoever Things are True: *Discourses on Truth* by J.H. Thornwell
The Word & Prayer: *Devotions from Minor Prophets* by John Calvin

Call us Toll Free at 1-877-666-9469
Send us an e-mail at sgcb@charter.net
Visit us on line at solid-ground-books.com

www.ingramcontent.com/pod-product-compliance
Lightning Source LLC
LaVergne TN
LVHW041622070426
835507LV00008B/400